List of Contents

Introduction

In a world that's constantly evolving, there's a relentless march toward digitalization. It's a realm where traditional boundaries and limitations no longer apply, and the concept of a brick-and-mortar storefront has become almost archaic. The digital landscape is an ever-expanding realm of endless possibilities, limited only by the scope of your imagination.

Welcome to the world of digital business, where your business begins with the realization that the only constant is change. A world where your potential to create, innovate, and prosper knows no bounds. This book is your guide to navigating the uncharted waters of building a digital business from scratch to success, all while maintaining a firm grip on the reins of cost-effectiveness.

In the days of past, setting up a business meant securing a physical location, dealing with inventory, and investing a significant amount of capital. But in this digital era, the paradigm has shifted. You no longer need a brick-and-mortar establishment to start a thriving enterprise. The foundation of the digital business world is not cement, steel, or wood; it's the virtual infrastructure that allows you to connect with a global audience in the blink of an eye.

The magic of digital business lies in its accessibility. Anyone with an internet connection and a computer can participate. The cost barriers are virtually non-existent, making it possible for aspiring entrepreneurs to follow their dreams without plunging deep into debt.

So, what is a digital business? In its simplest form, it's a business that operates primarily online. Whether you're selling products, offering services, or creating content, your digital business can take many forms. It's the e-commerce store that operates 24/7, the blog that educates and entertains, or the software application that simplifies everyday tasks.

But this book isn't about simply existing in the digital realm; it's about thriving and succeeding. You might be thinking, "If it's that easy, everyone would be doing it." True, the digital sphere is filled with opportunities, but it's also fraught with competition. Success in this world demands a combination of innovation, dedication, and smart strategy.

Digital business is a vast landscape, much like the cosmos itself, with countless stars shining in the form of websites, apps, and online platforms. Yet, every one of these digital stars is unique, much like you. You hold the potential to shine brighter than the rest, to carve your own path in this digital galaxy.

As you explore this book, let's debunk the myth that starting a digital business requires hefty financial investments. This isn't about writing blank checks, but about judiciously allocating your resources. In the following pages, you'll discover innovative methods to reduce costs while maximizing returns. We'll show you how to transform your creative ideas into reality without breaking the bank.

The principles outlined in this book are not just theories and conjectures. They are based on solid research and the experiences of countless individuals who have ventured into the digital realm. It's not a get-rich-quick scheme, but a roadmap to sustainable success.

Success in the digital world isn't defined by mere survival; it's about thriving in an ever-changing landscape. The strategies you'll learn here are not just about building a business; they are about building a legacy. Digital business isn't a sprint; it's a marathon. This isn't about taking shortcuts; it's about finding the most efficient path.

Think of your digital business as a plant. In the beginning, it needs nurturing, care, and attention to grow. But as it matures, it becomes a resilient tree that can withstand the storms of competition, the droughts of market fluctuations, and the challenges of technological evolution.

This book isn't just a manual for creating a digital business; it's a manifesto for embracing the future. The future of business is digital, and it's time to seize the opportunities it presents. It's time to embrace the principles of frugality and innovation that make digital business not only possible but also thriving.

You don't need deep pockets or a vast network to succeed in the digital realm. What you need is a deep understanding of your niche, a clear vision of your business, and the unwavering determination to make it happen.

This is your opportunity to embrace a new way of doing business. The digital world offers a level playing field, where you compete not by the size of your capital but by the strength of your ideas and the quality of your execution. Success in the digital world isn't reserved for a select few; it's open to anyone who is willing to learn, adapt, and persevere.

In the pages that follow, you'll uncover the secrets to building a digital business from scratch and scaling it to new heights—all with minimal costs. You'll learn how to identify profitable niches, create high-value digital products, and market your business effectively. You'll discover the art of customer acquisition, retention, and monetization.

Success in the digital world is within your grasp. The only question is, are you ready to seize it? This book is your roadmap to success. It's time to dive into the exciting world of digital business.

Chapter 1: Introduction to the Digital Business World

1.1 Understanding Digital Business

In the modern economy, the term "digital business" has become more than just a fantasy; it's a fundamental concept that underpins the way we live and work. This section sets the stage for our journey into the world of digital entrepreneurship. We will delve into what digital business means, how it has reshaped our economic landscape, and why it has emerged as a powerful alternative to traditional business models.

Defining Digital Business and Its Impact on the Modern Economy

To start, let's define what we mean by "digital business." Simply put, a digital business is an enterprise that primarily operates in the digital realm. It leverages digital technologies and the internet to deliver products, services, or information to customers. Unlike traditional brick-and-mortar businesses, digital businesses don't rely on physical storefronts or extensive infrastructure. Instead, they harness the power of the virtual world to connect with their audience.

The impact of digital business on the modern economy cannot be overstated. It has ushered in a new era of commerce, enabling businesses to transcend geographical boundaries, reach global audiences, and operate 24/7. This transformation has brought about a seismic shift in how we conduct trade, interact with customers, and create value. Digital business models have disrupted industries, challenged established norms, and democratized entrepreneurship.

Consider the rise of e-commerce giants like Amazon, which have redefined the way we shop, or the rapid expansion of the gig economy, offering flexible work opportunities that were unimaginable a few decades ago. These are just a couple of examples showcasing how digital business has penetrated nearly every aspect of our lives, from how we consume media to how we manage our finances.

The Rise of Digital Entrepreneurship
As digital business models have gained prominence, so too has the concept of digital entrepreneurship. Traditional entrepreneurship often conjures images of individuals opening physical stores, manufacturing products, or providing local services. Digital entrepreneurship, on the other hand, represents a shift toward virtual, online, and tech-driven enterprises.

Digital entrepreneurs are the pioneers of this new frontier, charting a course into uncharted territory. They are individuals who recognize the boundless potential of the digital realm and harness it to create, innovate, and solve problems. Their tools are not brick and mortar, but lines of code, cloud servers, and an unwavering vision for the digital landscape. Digital entrepreneurs are the architects of change, constantly adapting to emerging technologies and evolving consumer demands.

In the past, entrepreneurship may have required substantial capital, physical infrastructure, and a network of business connections. Digital entrepreneurship, however, has leveled the playing field. It allows aspiring entrepreneurs to enter the market with minimal overhead costs. All that's needed is a computer, internet access, and a willingness to learn, adapt, and grow.

The rise of digital entrepreneurship has not only democratized business ownership but also created new opportunities for those who may have been excluded or overlooked in traditional business circles. It's a vehicle for economic empowerment and a means to escape the limitations of a 9-to-5 job. In the digital world, anyone with a passion, a good idea, and the determination to execute can become an entrepreneur.

The Advantages of Digital Business Over Traditional Models

One of the central themes of this book is the idea that digital business offers distinct advantages over traditional models. Let's explore some of these advantages in more detail:

1. Cost Efficiency: Unlike traditional businesses that often require significant capital for rent, inventory, and staff, digital businesses can be launched with minimal upfront costs. With the right approach, you can start your digital

venture with little to no initial investment, making entrepreneurship more accessible than ever.

2. Global Reach: Digital businesses are not confined by geographical borders. The internet enables you to connect with a worldwide audience, tapping into markets and demographics that were once out of reach. This global reach allows for rapid expansion and growth.

3. Flexibility and Accessibility: Digital businesses offer flexibility in terms of work hours and location. You're not tied to a physical office, and many digital entrepreneurs enjoy the freedom of working from anywhere with an internet connection. This flexibility can lead to a healthier work-life balance.

4. Data-Driven Decision Making: The digital environment provides a wealth of data and analytics tools that allow you to understand your customers, track your business's performance, and make informed decisions. Data-driven insights enable you to adapt and refine your strategies in real-time.

5. Scalability: Digital businesses can scale quickly and efficiently. As demand for your products or services grows, you can expand without the logistical challenges often associated with traditional businesses. Scaling a digital business can be as simple as adding more server capacity or hiring additional virtual team members.

6. Reduced Overhead: Without the need for physical storefronts, inventory, or extensive office space, digital businesses can keep their overhead costs to a minimum.

This cost-efficiency can translate into higher profit margins and reinvestment opportunities.

The advantages of digital business go beyond these points, but these are some of the fundamental reasons why individuals and organizations are increasingly turning to digital entrepreneurship. Whether you're looking to start a side hustle, transition to a new career, or build a global brand, the digital business world provides an abundance of opportunities.

1.2 The Promise of Zero-Cost Digital Ventures

Starting a business is often perceived as a monumental task, one that requires deep pockets and significant financial investments. Common myths surround the idea that launching a successful business inevitably involves substantial startup costs. This perception, however, couldn't be further from the truth, especially in the realm of digital business.

Debunking Common Myths About Startup Costs

Myth 1: "You Need a Pile of Money to Start"

The misconception that to start a business, one must empty their bank account and gather piles of cash is a prevalent one. This notion discourages many aspiring entrepreneurs from even taking the first step. The reality is that the digital age has ushered in a new era of business, where financial barriers are not as formidable as they once were. You can venture into the world of digital business without breaking the bank.

Myth 2: "You Must Secure Substantial Loans or Investors"

Another myth that frequently discourages potential business owners is the belief that you need deep-pocketed investors or substantial loans to get your business off the ground. While securing investment or loans can be beneficial for some businesses, the idea that it's a mandatory step is misleading. In the digital business landscape, it's entirely possible to build a profitable enterprise with minimal or no external financial support.

Myth 3: "Quality Requires High Spending"

Some might argue that cost-saving strategies inevitably lead to subpar quality. However, in the digital world, creativity and ingenuity can lead to high-quality outcomes without a hefty price tag. This chapter will show you how to maximize quality while keeping costs to a minimum.

The Value of Innovative Cost-Saving Strategies

In the digital business world, innovative thinking and resourcefulness are prized above all else. Traditional businesses often involve substantial overheads – rent, utilities, physical inventory – but digital businesses benefit from a landscape of low-cost, high-impact opportunities. The key lies in harnessing the power of technology, leveraging free or affordable tools, and utilizing your own skills to reduce expenses.

The Potential for High Returns Without a Large Initial Investment

Imagine this: You have a brilliant idea, a passion for a particular niche, and the determination to succeed. In the digital business world, these assets are worth their weight in gold. The potential for high returns without a large initial investment is the promise that the digital realm holds.

The digital sphere has become the great equalizer in the business world. It levels the playing field, allowing innovative, dedicated individuals to compete with even the most established corporations. By leveraging the tools, strategies, and insights that this book will unfold, you can unlock the door to high returns without a massive upfront investment.

Consider this: With a computer, an internet connection, and your ideas, you have the foundation for your digital venture. You don't need to purchase a fleet of delivery trucks, rent office space, or stock a warehouse full of physical products. The beauty of digital business lies in its minimal overhead costs.

And here's the fascinating part: Many digital entrepreneurs begin their journey as solopreneurs. They're one-person armies, using their creativity and innovation to build businesses from scratch. As you'll learn in this book, it's entirely feasible to keep costs to a minimum while scaling your digital business and watching the profits grow.

In the world of zero-cost digital ventures, your success is defined not by the depth of your pockets, but by the depth of your determination and the breadth of your knowledge. It's about crafting a unique proposition, identifying opportunities, and smartly leveraging the resources available at your fingertips.

While we won't promise that building a digital business is easy, we will assert that it's entirely possible, and the rewards can be substantial. Remember that while it's not free of effort, it is free of the exorbitant costs that once barred so many from the world of entrepreneurship.

1.3 Setting Your Vision for Success

The landscape of business has undergone a seismic shift. Traditional models have given way to a dynamic, technology-driven arena that offers boundless opportunities for those who dare to venture into the digital realm. If you're reading this, it's likely you're one of the daring entrepreneurs ready to make your mark in the digital business world.

In the vast expanse of the digital business universe, clarity and foresight are your guiding stars. The first step is to establish a firm vision for your future. Your vision is your

Goal, the unwavering beacon that will guide every decision, every action, and every pivot along the way.

Defining Your Goals and Objectives

Begin by defining your goals and objectives with a precision that would make a surgeon proud. Your goals are the destination points on your digital map, while your objectives are the milestones you'll hit on your way there. When it comes to setting these markers, specificity is your ally. Don't merely aspire to 'be successful'; define success as it means to you. Maybe it's reaching a specific revenue figure, gaining a certain number of customers, or even making a profound difference in the world. It could be all of these. Make sure your goals are SMART—specific, measurable, achievable, relevant, and time-bound.

Consider a goal like "Within two years, I aim to generate $500,000 in revenue by providing 10,000 customers with a unique digital service that enhances their lives." It's specific, measurable, achievable, relevant, and comes with a clear timeframe. You can almost taste the success when your objectives are this well-defined.

Your goals and objectives are the coordinates on your roadmap, and they'll keep you on track even in the most turbulent digital storms.

Crafting a Clear Mission Statement

With your goals and objectives in place, it's time to craft a mission statement that encapsulates your purpose. Your mission statement is the soul of your digital business. It's not a mere tagline or a marketing gimmick; it's the essence of why your business exists. Think of it as the 'why' behind your 'what' and 'how.'

Let your mission statement be a crystalline reflection of your values, your passion, and the change you intend to bring into the world. It should resonate with your target audience, compelling them to join your digital journey. It must be clear and concise, a few lines that articulate your raison d'être.

For example, consider a mission statement like: "Our mission is to empower individuals with innovative, accessible, and zero-cost digital solutions that transform their lives and nurture a global community of informed, inspired, and connected change-makers."

With a mission statement like this, you're not just defining your purpose; you're aligning your digital business with a higher calling that resonates with the aspirations of your target audience. Your mission becomes your anchor, grounding you amidst the hustle and bustle of the digital world.

Identifying Your Target Audience and Market Niche

As you set your sights on the digital horizon, it's imperative to know who you're aiming to serve. Your target audience is your compass, directing you towards the individuals or groups who will benefit most from your digital offering. The more precise your understanding of your audience, the more effectively you can tailor your business to meet their needs.

Start by profiling your ideal customer. What are their demographics, preferences, challenges, and aspirations? Dig deep into their psychology and behaviors. You're not merely looking for 'a market' to serve; you're searching for the faces and voices of the people who will become your community, your champions, and your advocates.

Next, consider your market niche. This is where you'll plant your flag, your territory of expertise in the vast digital wilderness. What specific problem will you solve, what unique value will you bring, and what unmet need will you fulfill? Your niche is your domain of mastery, your space to excel, and your beachhead for success.

With this clear understanding of your target audience and market niche, you'll be poised to offer a digital solution that speaks directly to the hearts and minds of those who need it most. Your vision, goals, and mission become purposeful when aligned with the people you aim to serve.

Chapter 2: Niche Selection and Market Research

2.2 Finding Your Profitable Niche

To build a digital business, success hinges on a fundamental decision - finding the right niche. Your niche is the corner of the digital world that you'll carve out for yourself, where your expertise will shine, and your profits will grow. It's a pivotal choice that requires careful consideration, a blend of data-driven research, and a keen sense of your personal strengths and passions.

Researching Niche Opportunities

To kickstart your journey to success in the digital realm, the first step is to embark on a journey of research. You need to become a sleuth, investigating the vast digital landscape to unearth opportunities. The beauty of digital business is that it's an ever-evolving marketplace, constantly offering new openings for the astute entrepreneur. Here's how you can uncover your niche:

1. Market Analysis: Begin by scanning the digital horizon. What are the trends? Where is the demand growing? Investigate different sectors, industries, and markets. Research the latest developments, emerging technologies, and the evolving needs of the online audience. Dive into market reports, industry publications, and authoritative websites. This data-driven approach allows you to identify areas with untapped potential.

2. Keyword Research: The digital world communicates through keywords. Utilize powerful tools like Google Keyword Planner, SEMrush, or Ahrefs to identify the search terms that people are using. These keywords reveal the topics and niches that are in demand. Pay attention to search volume and competition levels. A niche with high demand and low competition is your golden ticket.

3. Social Media and Online Forums: Explore the vibrant conversations happening on social media platforms and niche-specific forums. Listen to what people are talking about, the questions they're asking, and the problems they're trying to solve. The insights from these interactions can help you find a niche that aligns with people's needs and interests.

4. Competitor Analysis: Your competition is an invaluable source of information. Study the businesses and entrepreneurs already active in your areas of interest. What niches are they thriving in? What strategies are they using? Analyzing your competitors can help you identify gaps in the market that you can fill with your unique approach.

Identifying Your Passion and Expertise
Choosing a niche isn't solely about following market trends; it's also about recognizing your own passion and expertise. Passion fuels your motivation, and expertise provides you with the necessary knowledge to stand out in a crowded digital landscape. Here's how to blend your personal strengths with niche selection:

1. Personal Interests: Start by listing your interests, hobbies, and topics that you are genuinely passionate about. Your enthusiasm for a subject can make the hard work of building a digital business feel more like a rewarding endeavor than a chore.

2. Skill Assessment: Identify your skills and expertise. What are you exceptionally good at? This could be your professional background, your unique talents, or even skills you've acquired over time. Your skills can set you apart in a competitive market.

3. Overlap Analysis: Look for an overlap between your passions and your expertise. When you find a niche where these two elements converge, you've discovered the sweet spot. Operating in a niche you're passionate about and knowledgeable in will not only make your work enjoyable but also give you a competitive edge.

Evaluating Market Demand and Competition
The last piece of the puzzle is evaluating the niche's demand and the level of competition you'll face. It's crucial to strike a balance between a niche that you're passionate about and one that offers a reasonable chance of success. Here's how to assess the profitability of your chosen niche:

1. Demand Metrics: Utilize the data you've gathered from market research and keyword analysis to determine the demand for your chosen niche. Are people actively searching for information, products, or services related to it? Look for consistent patterns of demand over time.

2. Competition Analysis: Investigate the competition in your niche. High competition can make it challenging for newcomers, while low competition can indicate a lack of demand. A healthy niche often has a moderate level of competition. Analyze your potential competitors' strengths and weaknesses to identify opportunities.

3. Monetization Potential: Consider the monetization opportunities within your niche. Are there products or services that can be sold? Can you create valuable content that people are willing to pay for? Evaluate the income potential and profit margins to ensure your chosen niche can be financially rewarding.

In your quest to find the perfect niche, the ideal balance is a niche that aligns with your passions and expertise, exhibits strong market demand, and offers reasonable competition. Remember that your chosen niche will serve as the foundation for your entire digital business. So, take your time, be thorough in your research, and choose wisely. Once you've found that sweet spot, you'll be on your way to building a successful zero-cost digital business from scratch.

2.2 Conducting In-Depth Market Research

In the digital business, one cannot overstate the importance of thorough market research. This is the backbone upon which you'll build your empire—a meticulous understanding of the environment in which your business operates. In this section, we will dive into the core components of conducting in-depth market research: exploring market trends and consumer behavior, analyzing competitor strengths and weaknesses, and discovering untapped opportunities within your niche.

Exploring Market Trends and Consumer Behavior
Market trends and consumer behavior are the compass guiding your business towards its true north. Before you embark on your digital entrepreneurial journey, take the time to understand the currents of your chosen niche. This is not merely an academic exercise; it's a practical necessity.

Market trends are like the ever-changing tides of the digital sea. These trends represent shifts in consumer preferences, technology advancements, and broader socioeconomic factors that can significantly impact your business. To stay ahead, monitor and analyze these trends continuously. Utilize market research tools, industry reports, and expert insights to keep your finger on the pulse.

Consumer behavior is the cornerstone of your market understanding. It's a lens through which you perceive your target audience's motivations, desires, and pain points. By understanding what makes your potential customers tick, you can tailor your product or service to meet their needs.

So, how can you delve into consumer behavior effectively? Start with surveys and questionnaires. These can provide valuable insights into your target audience's preferences and pain points. Additionally, leverage analytics tools to study user interactions on your website or app. This can reveal patterns and behaviors that are otherwise hidden.

Moreover, don't forget to explore social media and online communities related to your niche. Here, you can engage in direct conversations with potential customers, gaining a deeper understanding of their thoughts and desires. By dissecting the data from these sources, you'll not only identify your target audience but also tailor your offerings to address their specific needs.

Analyzing Competitor Strengths and Weaknesses
The digital business arena is no empty field; it's a bustling marketplace with numerous players vying for attention. And this competition can be your best teacher. By studying the strengths and weaknesses of your competitors, you can craft a strategic advantage for your own business.

Begin by identifying your direct competitors. Who are they, and what do they offer that's similar to your product or service? Analyze their websites, customer reviews, and social media profiles. What do customers like about their offerings, and what complaints do they have? Understanding the gaps and opportunities in their offerings will give you a competitive edge.

Examine their marketing strategies. Are they utilizing content marketing, social media, or paid advertising? What's their approach, and how effective is it? This information will help you refine your own marketing strategy to stand out in a crowded market.

But, don't stop at just your direct competitors. Cast a wider net to identify indirect competitors—businesses offering related products or services. Analyzing them can reveal untapped niches or opportunities for partnerships that could enhance your offerings.

Discovering Untapped Opportunities Within Your Niche

The world of digital business is not static; it's dynamic and ever-evolving. Even within well-established niches, there are often unexplored corners and fresh opportunities waiting to be discovered.

Your research should go beyond the surface. To identify these untapped opportunities, keep your ear to the ground and your finger on the pulse. Pay attention to emerging trends and technologies that might disrupt or enhance your niche. Consider the changing demographics of your target audience and how it may affect their preferences and needs.

Moreover, look for gaps in your competitors' offerings. Are there areas where they're falling short, leaving room for improvement or innovation? By identifying these gaps, you can position your business to fill them, providing a solution where others have fallen short.

Sometimes, these opportunities can stem from customer feedback or requests. Listen to your potential customers. What are they asking for that they currently can't find in the market? By actively seeking and responding to customer input, you not only address their needs but also gain a competitive advantage by being attentive and responsive.

Conducting in-depth market research is not just a preliminary step—it's an ongoing process. Stay vigilant and adapt to changes in market trends, understand your consumers at a granular level, and keep an eagle eye on your competitors and untapped opportunities. This deep understanding will be the cornerstone upon which you build and fortify your digital business, setting the stage for long-term success.

2.3 Validating Your Niche Choice

In the world of zero-cost digital business, your niche selection is a pivotal determinant of your success. It's not a matter of throwing darts blindly at a board; rather, it requires a methodical approach, precise aim, and the tools to gauge whether you're on target. This section explores the crucial task of validating your niche choice, a fundamental step to ensure your digital enterprise's viability and longevity.

Testing Your Niche with a Minimum Viable Product

Before committing to a niche, it's imperative to create a minimum viable product (MVP) to test the waters. Think of an MVP as a litmus test for your niche concept. It's a streamlined version of your product or service, designed to answer fundamental questions. Will your audience find value in what you're offering? Is your chosen niche indeed in demand?

The MVP is not about bells and whistles; it's about providing a core solution that addresses a specific problem within your chosen niche. This stripped-down version allows you to allocate your limited resources judiciously and gather valuable insights without investing heavily. Here's how to go about it:

1. Define Your MVP Objectives: Start by setting clear, achievable goals for your MVP. What do you aim to learn or validate with this initial product or service? For example, if you plan to offer an online course in the niche of personal finance, your MVP might consist of a single module or lesson, designed to test the appetite for such content.

2. Build the Bare Minimum: Strip away all unnecessary features, design elements, or content. Focus on delivering the essential value to your target audience. This might mean a basic webpage, a free e-book, or a simplified version of your software tool.

3. Launch and Collect Data: Introduce your MVP to your intended audience, whether through a website, social media, or email marketing. Monitor user interactions, gather feedback, and track metrics. Pay attention to user engagement, conversion rates, and feedback from users. Are they signing up? Are they finding value in your offering? Their behavior will tell you if you're onto something.

4. Adapt and Iterate: Based on the data and feedback you've collected, adapt your MVP. This might involve improving the user experience, enhancing content, or even changing your niche direction. The key is to be agile in response to the market's signals.

Collecting Feedback and Making Data-Driven Decisions

In the digital realm, data is your North Star. It's not a crystal ball, but it's the next best thing, offering a clearer view of your niche's viability. To validate your niche choice, you must be proactive in collecting and interpreting data. Here's how:

1. Utilize Analytics Tools: Embrace web analytics, email marketing analytics, and social media insights. These tools provide invaluable data on user behavior, traffic sources, conversion rates, and more. They give you a pulse on what's working and what's not.

2. Engage with Your Audience: Encourage your audience to provide feedback. Surveys, online forms, and direct communication channels are your allies. You want to understand their pain points, preferences, and expectations.

3. Monitor Competitors: Keep a watchful eye on your niche competitors. What are they doing right? What are they missing? Analyzing their strategies can provide insights into unmet needs and opportunities.

4. A/B Testing: Implement A/B testing on your digital assets, such as landing pages, ad campaigns, or email

subject lines. By comparing two versions of a web page or content piece, you can gauge which resonates better with your audience, helping refine your approach.

Ensuring Long-Term Sustainability in Your Chosen Niche

In the fast-paced world of digital business, staying power is invaluable. To ensure the long-term sustainability of your chosen niche, consider the following strategies:

1. Build a Brand Identity: Establish a unique brand that resonates with your target audience. Your brand should communicate your values, expertise, and the value you bring to your niche. You can read more this on the book "Branding Brilliance: Crafting a Memorable Brand Identity that Resonates"

2. Diversify and Innovate: Don't rest on your laurels. Continue to innovate and diversify your offerings within your niche. Adapt to changing market trends and emerging technologies.

3. Community Building: Foster a community around your niche. Engage with your audience through social media, forums, or webinars. A dedicated community can be a powerful support system and source of feedback.

4. Content Quality and Consistency: Maintain high-quality content and a consistent publishing schedule. Providing valuable, updated content keeps your audience engaged and returning for more.

5. Stay Informed: Stay informed about developments in your niche, industry, and the broader digital landscape. Knowledge is power, and being aware of shifts in the digital landscape can help you adapt and stay relevant.

The steps to validating your niche choice involves rigorous testing, data-driven decision-making, and a commitment to long-term sustainability. It's about listening to your audience, interpreting the data, and adapting your strategy based on what you learn. By following these steps, you increase your chances of building a zero-cost digital business that not only survives but thrives in your chosen niche.

Chapter 3: Creating Your Digital Product or Service

3.1 Product Development Strategies

In the world of zero-cost digital business, the foundation of your enterprise lies in your product or service. This is the essence of your venture, the solution you provide, and the value you bring to your target audience. In this section, we dive deep into product development strategies that will not only help you create something extraordinary but also set you apart from the crowd.

Choosing the Right Product or Service Type

Selecting the right product or service type is a critical decision that will shape the direction of your digital business. It's about more than just what you're passionate about; it's about what your audience needs and craves. Here, we dissect the process and factors that should guide your choice.

Understanding Your Audience

Before you can decide what to offer, you must thoroughly understand your target audience. Who are they? What are their pain points? What problems do they need solving? To create a product or service that resonates, you must first speak their language.

Market Research and Niche Analysis

Market research isn't just something to be checked off a list; it's an ongoing, integral part of your digital business's life. By identifying gaps in the market and analyzing competitors, you'll find opportunities to create something unique that fills a need.

Leveraging Your Expertise and Passion

Passion is the driving force behind many successful digital businesses. It's not just about making money; it's about doing something you love. Your expertise and enthusiasm will shine through in your product or service and resonate with your audience.

Solving Real Problems

To stand out, you need to solve real, pressing problems. Don't just create for the sake of creation; make a difference in your audience's lives. A product or service that genuinely addresses their needs will be invaluable.

Developing a Unique Selling Proposition

Your Unique Selling Proposition (USP) is your secret weapon in the digital business world. It's the answer to the question, "Why should customers choose you over the competition?" In this section, we explore what a USP is and how to develop one that sets you apart.

Identifying Your Competitive Edge

Every business faces competition, but your competitive edge is what distinguishes you from the rest. It could be your unique expertise, innovative features, or unparalleled customer service. Identify your edge and make it the core of your USP.

Value Proposition: Meeting Your Customers' Needs

Your USP should align with your value proposition, which is essentially the promise you make to your customers. This is where you define the value they can expect to receive from your product or service. A strong, customer-centric value proposition is key to attracting and retaining clients.

Consistency and Reliability

A solid USP should reflect consistency and reliability. Can your audience trust that your product or service will deliver every time? Reliability can be a major selling point in a world where customers are often skeptical about new offerings.

Prototyping and Iteration

Once you've defined your product or service and established your USP, it's time to get your hands dirty and start building. But keep in mind, your first iteration is unlikely to be perfect. In this section, we explore the importance of prototyping and iteration.

The Power of Prototyping

Prototyping is the art of creating a simplified version of your product or service, a blueprint that allows you to visualize and test your idea. It's a way to iron out the kinks and discover potential flaws before you invest significant resources.

Testing and Feedback

Your prototype isn't set in stone. You should actively seek feedback from potential users and stakeholders. This feedback loop is invaluable in refining your product or service to meet the actual needs and expectations of your audience.

The Iteration Process

Iteration is a continuous, incremental improvement of your product or service. As you gather feedback and learn from your initial attempts, you apply those lessons to make your offering better. This cycle of improvement is the path to excellence.

The Beauty of Flexibility

In a zero-cost digital business, you have the advantage of being nimble and adaptable. Your low overhead allows you to pivot and adjust as you go, responding to market demands and customer feedback in real-time.

Your product or service is the cornerstone of your digital business. It must solve real problems, resonate with your audience, and have a Unique Selling Proposition that sets you apart from the competition. Once you've defined these elements, don't be afraid to prototype, test, and iterate. This approach will help you refine your offering, making it more valuable and marketable. Remember, in the digital business world, it's the tangible value you provide that ultimately leads to your success.

3.2 Crafting High-Quality Content

In the realm of digital business, crafting high-quality content stands as a cornerstone of success. It's not merely about churning out words, images, or videos; it's about delivering value, engaging your audience, and leaving a lasting impression. In this section, we will delve into the core aspects of content creation, understanding what it takes to produce content that resonates with your audience, elevates your brand, and ultimately drives success.

Content Creation Essentials

Effective content creation starts with a fundamental understanding of what your audience needs and wants. It's about empathizing with their challenges, questions, and desires.

1. Know Your Audience: The first and foremost step in crafting high-quality content is to intimately know your audience. Who are they? What are their pain points? What keeps them up at night? By conducting thorough market research and creating detailed buyer personas, you can tailor your content to address their specific needs.

2. Content Strategy: Crafting content without a strategy is akin to embarking on a road trip without a map. Develop a content strategy that outlines your goals, the type of content you'll create, and how it aligns with your business objectives. This strategy provides a roadmap, ensuring every piece of content serves a purpose and contributes to your overarching mission.

3. Keyword Research: In the digital landscape, keywords are the compass that guides your content to the right audience. Through comprehensive keyword research, you can identify the terms and phrases your target audience is searching for. Integrating these keywords into your content ensures it's discoverable by those who need it.

4. Value-Driven Content: Quality content is content that provides value. Whether it's solving a problem, answering a question, or simply entertaining, each piece should leave the reader or viewer feeling that their time was well-spent.

Prioritize educating, informing, or entertaining your audience in each content piece.

5. Originality and Uniqueness: While it's essential to draw inspiration from existing content, the true mark of excellence is originality. Don't just rehash what others have said. Offer a unique perspective, insight, or approach that sets your content apart. Remember, your voice and your brand's personality are integral elements in creating that uniqueness.

Leveraging Multimedia and Storytelling
Multimedia, including images, videos, infographics, and interactive content, plays a pivotal role in content creation. In the digital age, multimedia elements are not just optional but often expected by your audience.

1. Visual Storytelling: Visual content is a powerful medium for storytelling. Humans are naturally drawn to visuals, and incorporating them into your content can enhance engagement. Whether it's through striking images, well-designed infographics, or compelling videos, each element should complement and enhance the narrative.

2. Video Content: The surge of video content in recent years has been nothing short of remarkable. Video offers a dynamic way to connect with your audience, whether through product demonstrations, how-to guides, or compelling brand stories. The key is to keep it relevant and focused, ensuring viewers are captivated from the start.

3. Infographics and Data Visualization: Complex information is often best conveyed through infographics and data visualization. These tools allow you to simplify intricate data or concepts, making them accessible and engaging for your audience.

4. Interactive Content: Interactive content, such as quizzes, polls, and interactive guides, not only engages the audience but also offers a unique way to gather data and feedback. It's a two-way street that can foster a deeper connection with your audience.

5. Storytelling: Storytelling is a timeless art that remains as relevant in the digital world as it ever was. Weaving compelling narratives into your content can captivate your audience, create emotional connections, and leave a lasting impression. Stories have the power to humanize your brand, making it relatable and memorable.

Maintaining Consistency and Quality

Maintaining the quality and consistency of your content is a testament to your commitment to your audience and your brand. This is where many digital businesses falter – they start strong but struggle to sustain the momentum.

1. Content Calendar: A content calendar is your organization's best friend. It provides a structured overview of what content you will produce, when it will be published, and who is responsible for its creation. Consistency in posting and adhering to your schedule ensures that your audience knows what to expect.

2. Quality Assurance: Never compromise on quality. It's better to have less content of high quality than more content of lower quality. Maintain high standards through editing, proofreading, and fact-checking. Your audience trusts you to provide reliable information, and quality control is paramount to that trust.

3. Feedback Loop: Invite and listen to feedback. Feedback from your audience, as well as your team, is invaluable for improvement. It can help you understand what's working, what's not, and what needs adjustment. Use data analytics and feedback mechanisms to continuously fine-tune your content strategy.

Crafting high-quality content is not a one-time task; it's an ongoing steps to delivering value, engaging your audience, and fostering brand loyalty. By understanding your audience, leveraging multimedia, and maintaining quality and consistency, you'll be on the path to creating content that truly resonates and drives your digital business towards success.

3.3 Legal and Ethical Considerations

In the world of digital entrepreneurship, as in any business, legality and ethics are essential pillars that underpin your operations. Focusing on this foundation from the outset is not merely a compliance obligation but a strategic decision that can help you avoid pitfalls and foster trust with your customers. This section delves into three crucial facets of the legal and ethical landscape in the digital realm: intellectual property and copyrights, privacy and data protection, and compliance with digital business regulations.

Intellectual Property and Copyrights

Intellectual property (IP) is the bedrock of many digital businesses. It encompasses the creations of your mind, such as inventions, literary and artistic works, and symbols, names, and images used in commerce. Protecting your IP is paramount, as it not only safeguards your unique ideas but also maintains the integrity of your brand and offering.

One key aspect of IP protection is copyright. Copyright grants you exclusive rights to your original literary and artistic works. These can include written content, graphics, software code, music, and more. As you embark on creating your digital product or service, keep these copyright considerations in mind:

1. Ownership and Authorship: Determine who holds the rights to the content you produce. If you work with freelancers or collaborators, establish clear contracts outlining the ownership of the intellectual property.

2. Fair Use: Familiarize yourself with the concept of "fair use" in copyright law. This doctrine allows limited use of copyrighted material without permission for purposes such as criticism, commentary, news reporting, teaching, scholarship, and research.

3. Licensing: Understand the various types of licenses you can apply to your work. Licensing allows you to specify how others can use your content while retaining ownership. Creative Commons licenses, for example, offer a spectrum of permissions to creators.

4. Plagiarism and Attribution: Acknowledge the importance of giving proper attribution to sources and creators. Avoid plagiarism, and encourage ethical content sharing.

Copyright infringement can lead to legal repercussions, so it's wise to ensure that your content is not infringing on others' rights. While the internet is a vast sea of information, intellectual property rights remain an essential safeguard for your digital business's integrity.

Privacy and Data Protection

With the increasing focus on privacy and data protection, understanding and adhering to relevant laws and regulations is not just a legal requirement but a foundation of trust in the digital realm. As you craft your digital product or service, consider these essential elements:

1. User Consent: Ensure that you obtain informed consent from your users regarding the collection and use of their personal data. This is particularly crucial if your business involves data collection or personalization.

2. Transparency: Be transparent about your data practices. Clearly state how user data will be used, stored, and who it may be shared with.

3. Data Security: Prioritize data security. Implement robust security measures to protect user data from breaches, unauthorized access, and cyber threats.

4. Legal Compliance: Comply with international data protection regulations like GDPR (General Data Protection Regulation) in Europe or CCPA (California Consumer Privacy Act) in the United States, depending on your audience and location.

5. Data Retention: Establish data retention policies that outline how long user data will be stored. Avoid keeping data longer than necessary.

Remember that privacy is not only a legal requirement but also a significant factor in user trust. Respecting your users' privacy will go a long way in building credibility for your digital business.

Compliance with Digital Business Regulations

The digital landscape is a dynamic and ever-evolving space, and staying compliant with relevant regulations is crucial to avoiding legal entanglements. Compliance ensures that you're operating within the boundaries set by governments and industry-specific bodies. Here's how to navigate these waters effectively:

1. Research Regulations: Stay informed about the specific regulations that pertain to your industry and location. For instance, e-commerce businesses often face different requirements than online content platforms.

2. Business Structure: Choose a business structure that aligns with your long-term goals and complies with the legal framework of your location. This might include considerations like registering as a sole proprietorship, LLC, or corporation.

3. Licenses and Permits: Determine if your digital business requires any licenses or permits. Different types of businesses may need different regulatory approvals.

4. Terms of Service and Privacy Policy: Create clear and comprehensive terms of service and privacy policies for your website or app. These documents should detail user rights and responsibilities and compliance with relevant laws.

5. Taxation and Reporting: Understand the tax obligations specific to your business. This includes income tax, sales tax, and reporting requirements.

6. Accessibility: Ensure that your digital products and services are accessible to individuals with disabilities, in compliance with accessibility laws such as the Americans with Disabilities Act (ADA).

Remember, non-compliance can lead to hefty fines, legal troubles, and reputational damage. By integrating these legal and ethical considerations into your digital business strategy from the outset, you're not only safeguarding your enterprise but also building a reputation as an honest and responsible operator in the digital sphere.

The process of creating your digital product or service is an exciting and transformative phase of your zero-cost digital business journey. However, amidst the creative process and entrepreneurial spirit, it's paramount to establish a strong legal and ethical foundation. Understanding the nuances of intellectual property, privacy and data protection, and compliance with digital business regulations will not only keep you on the right side of the law but also instill trust and confidence in your users. As you proceed with building your digital offering, always remember that legality and ethics are not just legal checkboxes; they're the backbones of a successful and sustainable digital enterprise.

Chapter 4: Zero-Cost Marketing Strategies

4.1 Content Marketing and SEO

In the digital realm, where information is at the tip of everyone's fingers, the key to success lies in being seen, heard, and remembered. One of the most powerful tools at your disposal for this endeavor is Content Marketing, paired with Search Engine Optimization (SEO). These twin engines drive the online success of countless businesses, big and small. In this section, we'll delve into the nitty-gritty of content marketing and SEO, giving you a comprehensive understanding of how to leverage them effectively without breaking the bank.

Creating Valuable Content

Content is the backbone of your digital presence. It's the lifeblood that attracts, engages, and retains your audience. But not just any content will suffice. It must be valuable. Valuable content is the gold standard in the digital world, the kind that not only keeps your audience coming back for more but also draws new eyes to your digital doorstep. But what is valuable content, and how can you create it?

Valuable content is informative, relevant, and tailored to your target audience. It's content that answers their questions, solves their problems, or entertains them. It provides real value, enriching their lives in some way. Here are the key points to consider when creating valuable content:

1. Understanding Your Audience: Before you even think about creating content, it's crucial to understand your audience. What are their pain points, desires, and needs? Research your target demographic thoroughly, and create content that resonates with them.

2. Quality Over Quantity: It's not about churning out content in massive quantities. It's about creating high-quality content that genuinely helps your audience. This might be in the form of in-depth articles, how-to guides, informative videos, or engaging podcasts.

3. Consistency: Building an audience takes time and consistency. Create a content schedule and stick to it. Consistency builds trust with your audience, and they'll come to rely on you for valuable insights.

4. Storytelling: Everyone loves a good story. Weave storytelling into your content to make it relatable and engaging. Stories create an emotional connection with your audience.

Search Engine Optimization Techniques
While creating valuable content is the first crucial step, it's equally vital that your content is discoverable. This is where Search Engine Optimization, or SEO, comes into play. SEO is the practice of optimizing your online content to be found and ranked higher by search engines like Google. It's your ticket to improving your website's visibility and attracting organic traffic. Let's dive into some fundamental SEO techniques:

1. Keyword Research: Start by researching and identifying keywords related to your content. These are the words and phrases your target audience is likely to use when searching for information online. Use keyword research tools to find the most relevant and frequently searched terms.

2. On-Page Optimization: Incorporate your chosen keywords naturally into your content, including titles, headings, and throughout the body. Make sure your content is well-structured and easy to read.

3. Meta Tags: Craft compelling meta titles and descriptions for your web pages and blog posts. These are the snippets that appear in search engine results, so they need to be attention-grabbing and descriptive.

4. Quality Backlinks: Building high-quality backlinks to your content is a powerful SEO strategy. When reputable websites link to your content, it signals to search engines that your content is valuable and trustworthy.

5. Mobile Optimization: Ensure your website is mobile-friendly. With the increasing use of smartphones, search engines favor mobile-optimized sites.

Leveraging Keywords and Analytics

Keywords are the breadcrumbs leading search engine users to your content. But it's not just about using keywords; it's about leveraging them intelligently. This involves strategically integrating keywords into your content while maintaining a natural flow. Here's how to make the most of keywords:

1. Long-Tail Keywords: Don't solely focus on generic, highly competitive keywords. Long-tail keywords are specific phrases that are easier to rank for and often bring in more targeted traffic. For example, instead of targeting "digital marketing," aim for something like "beginner's guide to digital marketing."

2. Keyword Placement: Place your primary keyword in your content's title and headings. Distribute related keywords naturally throughout the content.

3. Avoid Keyword Stuffing: Overloading your content with keywords can harm your SEO efforts. It's called keyword stuffing, and search engines penalize it. Keep your content readable and user-friendly.

Analytics are the compass that guides your content marketing and SEO strategies. They help you understand what's working, what's not, and where you can improve. The most common tool for this purpose is Google Analytics, which provides a wealth of data about your website's performance. Here are key aspects to monitor:

1. Traffic Sources: Understand where your website traffic is coming from. Is it primarily organic, social, or through referrals?

2. Audience Behavior: Analyze how visitors interact with your content. Which pages are most popular, and which ones have high bounce rates?

3. Conversion Tracking: Measure your success in terms of conversions, whether that's email sign-ups, product purchases, or other desired actions.

4. Keyword Performance: Track the performance of your chosen keywords. Are they driving traffic and conversions, or do you need to adjust your strategy?

5. Page Speed: A fast-loading website is essential for user experience and SEO. Slow-loading pages can result in high bounce rates.

By continually monitoring and adjusting your strategies based on analytics, you can refine your content marketing and SEO efforts, improving your online presence and reaching a wider audience. Remember, content marketing and SEO are ongoing processes that require dedication and adaptability.

Content marketing and SEO are twin pillars of zero-cost marketing that can significantly impact your digital business's success. Creating valuable content tailored to your audience, optimizing it for search engines, and using analytics to fine-tune your strategy are the key steps in this journey. By focusing on these fundamentals, you can build a strong online presence that attracts and retains a loyal following, all without breaking the bank.

4.2 Social Media and Community Building

In our digital world, establishing an influential online presence is not just an option; it's a necessity. Social media platforms have become the beating heart of the internet, connecting people, businesses, and ideas. In this section, we'll delve into the art of creating an engaging social media presence, nurturing online communities, and harnessing the potent force of user-generated content to boost your digital business—without breaking the bank.

Building an Engaging Social Media Presence

Social media isn't just a virtual water cooler for sharing cute cat videos and exchanging funny memes. It's a vibrant marketplace for building your brand, engaging with your audience, and showcasing your expertise. Your journey to social media success begins with choosing the right platforms. Don't spread yourself thin across every channel; focus on those that align with your target audience.

Now, the question is, how do you make a mark in the vast ocean of social media? The answer is simple: consistency and authenticity. Develop a consistent posting schedule, but remember that quality outweighs quantity. Offer valuable content that aligns with your niche, sharing industry insights, expert tips, and compelling visuals.

Additionally, don't overlook the power of human connection. Respond to comments, messages, and mentions. Engage in conversations, answer questions, and genuinely connect with your followers. This human touch sets you apart from faceless corporations and strengthens trust with your audience.

But what about the zero-cost aspect? Well, content creation doesn't have to drain your resources. Use free design tools like Canva for eye-catching graphics, and smartphone cameras can create remarkable visuals. User-generated

content is another treasure trove. Encourage your followers
to share their experiences with your product or service. It
not only showcases authenticity but also reduces your
content creation burden.

Building and Nurturing Online Communities

In the digital realm, communities are your allies. They're
the places where your brand can flourish, and your products
or services gain advocates. These communities might be
forums, Facebook groups, or even niche subreddits where
like-minded individuals gather. Join them. Become an
active participant and offer value without overtly pushing
your offerings.

Nurturing online communities requires respect and
humility. Never spam your links or products. Instead, foster
relationships by helping others and sharing your expertise.
When you become a valuable member of a community,
others are more likely to trust your brand.

Moreover, consistency is key. Show up regularly, engage in
discussions, and be respectful. Keep in mind that building a
strong community might take time, but the payoff in terms
of brand loyalty and word-of-mouth marketing is
immeasurable.

Harnessing the Power of User-Generated Content

User-generated content is a gift that keeps on giving. It's an
authentic and cost-effective way to showcase your products
or services through the eyes of satisfied customers.

Encourage your followers to share their experiences with your brand, whether it's a review, a photo, or a video.

Share these user-generated gems on your social media channels. This not only provides social proof but also shows your appreciation for your community. It's a win-win situation: your customers get the spotlight, and you get free promotion.

Additionally, user-generated content can provide valuable insights into your customers' experiences and needs. Listen to what they're saying, and use it to fine-tune your offerings. Customer feedback, especially when it's shared publicly, can be a goldmine of ideas for improvements and innovations.

Building an engaging social media presence, nurturing online communities, and harnessing user-generated content are pivotal components of your zero-cost marketing strategy. With consistency, authenticity, and a genuine connection to your audience, you can make a significant impact without a substantial financial investment.

4.3 Guerrilla Marketing and Growth Hacking

When marketing budgets can be tight and competition fierce, guerrilla marketing and growth hacking are two powerful weapons in your arsenal. These strategies empower you to achieve significant results without the need for extravagant advertising spending. In this section, we'll delve into creative, low-cost marketing tactics, explore ways to maximize growth through experimentation, and emphasize the importance of tracking and measuring your marketing efforts.

Creative, Low-Cost Marketing Tactics

When resources are limited, it's crucial to adopt innovative and unconventional marketing approaches. Guerrilla marketing, a term coined by Jay Conrad Levinson, focuses on thinking outside the box. It's about creating a big impact with minimal investment. Here are some creative, low-cost tactics that can help you stand out in a crowded digital marketplace.

1. Viral Content Creation: Viral content doesn't require a Hollywood budget. It's all about crafting shareable and attention-grabbing material that resonates with your target audience. Whether it's a witty meme, a captivating video, or a thought-provoking blog post, viral content can amplify your message without the need for hefty ad spend.

2. Social Media Stunts: Leveraging social media platforms can be a cost-effective way to engage with your audience. Creative social media stunts, like interactive quizzes, challenges, or user-generated content campaigns, can generate buzz and encourage user participation, all without a significant financial outlay.

3. Influencer Partnerships: Collaborating with micro-influencers in your niche can be a game-changer. Micro-influencers often have a highly engaged and loyal following. By forming partnerships, you can tap into their

audience, often at a fraction of the cost of partnering with major celebrities.

Maximizing Growth Through Experimentation

Growth hacking, a term popularized by Sean Ellis, is all about rapid experimentation and finding efficient ways to grow your user base. In the world of zero-cost digital business, embracing a growth hacking mindset can make all the difference.

1. A/B Testing: This is the cornerstone of growth hacking. By creating two or more variations of your content, landing pages, or email campaigns, you can test which one performs best. This data-driven approach allows you to optimize your strategies based on real user feedback.

2. Referral Programs: Encourage your existing customers to refer new ones by offering incentives or discounts. Dropbox, for instance, achieved exponential growth through a simple referral program, showing that creative approaches can lead to substantial results.

3. Landing Page Optimization: Your website's landing pages play a crucial role in converting visitors into customers. By continuously tweaking and optimizing these pages, you can increase your conversion rates over time.

Tracking and Measuring Your Marketing Efforts

In the digital business realm, tracking and measuring the effectiveness of your marketing efforts is non-negotiable.

Without this data, you're essentially navigating in the dark. Here's how you can ensure your marketing strategies are on the right track.

1. Analytics Tools: Utilize free or low-cost analytics tools like Google Analytics and social media insights to track website traffic, user behavior, and audience demographics. These tools provide valuable insights that inform your marketing decisions.

2. Key Performance Indicators (KPIs): Define and monitor KPIs that align with your business goals. These might include metrics such as conversion rates, click-through rates, customer acquisition cost, and customer lifetime value.

3. Data-Driven Decision-Making: The data you collect isn't just for show. It should drive your marketing strategy. Use the insights you gain to refine your approach, allocate resources more effectively, and experiment with new tactics.

Guerrilla marketing and growth hacking are dynamic, cost-effective strategies that can propel your zero-cost digital business to new heights. By harnessing creative marketing tactics, embracing experimentation, and diligently tracking your efforts, you can achieve remarkable results without breaking the bank. Remember, it's not about the size of your budget; it's about the size of your ideas and the effectiveness of your execution.

Chapter 5: Monetization Strategies and Revenue Generation

5.1 Developing Multiple Revenue Streams

In the world of digital business, revenue is the lifeblood of your operation. As you embark on your path to success, it's essential to explore various revenue streams to ensure a stable and thriving financial future. This section will delve into the crucial aspects of developing multiple revenue streams, diversifying your income sources, identifying affiliate marketing opportunities, and maximizing sales through upselling and cross-selling.

Diversifying Income Sources

Diversification isn't just a buzzword in the investment world; it's equally important in the realm of digital business. Relying on a single source of income can make your business vulnerable to market fluctuations and changes in consumer behavior. To mitigate this risk, consider the following strategies for diversifying your income sources:

1. Multiple Product or Service Offerings: Expanding your product or service line can significantly impact your income diversity. If you're currently offering a single digital product, consider developing complementary products or services that cater to your existing customer base or target audience.

2. Membership or Subscription Models: Implementing a subscription-based model can provide you with a steady

stream of recurring revenue. Offer exclusive content, features, or benefits to subscribers, enticing them to join and stay engaged.

3. Digital Merchandise: If your brand has a strong online presence, consider selling branded merchandise such as apparel, accessories, or digital downloads. This not only diversifies income but also acts as a marketing tool, strengthening brand recognition.

4. Consulting and Coaching: If you possess expertise in your niche, capitalize on it by offering consulting or coaching services. Many individuals and businesses are willing to pay for personalized guidance and insights.

5. Sponsored Content: Partner with relevant businesses or brands to create sponsored content. This can include product placements, sponsored articles, or co-branded promotions. Sponsored content can be a lucrative source of income while also expanding your reach.

Identifying Affiliate Marketing Opportunities
Affiliate marketing is a powerful tool in the digital business arsenal. It's a win-win situation where you promote other products or services, and in return, you earn a commission for every sale made through your referral. To identify and capitalize on affiliate marketing opportunities, follow these steps:

1. Niche Relevance: Choose affiliate products or services that align with your niche. Ensure they are relevant to your audience, as this increases the likelihood of conversions.

2. Product Research: Before promoting any product, conduct thorough research. Test the product yourself, read reviews, and evaluate the affiliate program's terms and conditions. You want to be confident in what you're promoting.

3. Transparency and Trust: Maintain transparency with your audience by disclosing your affiliate relationships. Building trust is crucial in affiliate marketing.

4. Content Integration: Create high-quality, informative content that seamlessly integrates affiliate links. Whether it's product reviews, tutorials, or recommendations, make sure the content provides value to your audience.

5. Testing and Optimization: Continuously monitor the performance of your affiliate links and optimize your approach. Experiment with different products, strategies, and placements to maximize your earnings.

Maximizing Sales through Upselling and Cross-Selling

To boost your revenue, you don't always need to attract new customers. Upselling and cross-selling are effective techniques for increasing the value of each transaction with existing customers. Here's how to make the most of these strategies:

1. Upselling: Upselling involves encouraging customers to purchase a more expensive or advanced version of the

product or service they initially intended to buy. To succeed in upselling, consider these tactics:

- Offer clear value: Highlight the additional benefits or features of the higher-priced option.

- Timing is key: Present the upsell at the right moment during the customer's journey, such as during checkout.

- Bundle deals: Create packages that combine the initial purchase with complementary items or services.

2. Cross-Selling: Cross-selling involves promoting related or complementary products or services to the one the customer is already buying. Implement these strategies for effective cross-selling:

- Understand customer needs: Analyze customer data and preferences to make relevant cross-selling recommendations.

- Personalize the offer: Tailor your cross-sell suggestions based on the customer's current purchase.

- Showcase the value: Clearly communicate how the additional product or service enhances the primary purchase.

Developing multiple revenue streams, identifying affiliate marketing opportunities, and maximizing sales through upselling and cross-selling are essential strategies for boosting the financial health of your digital business. By diversifying your income sources, you can reduce risk and ensure stability. Affiliate marketing can provide a steady stream of income while expanding your product or service offerings. Lastly, upselling and cross-selling are powerful techniques to increase revenue without acquiring additional customers. Implementing these strategies will help you create a robust and sustainable income structure for your digital business.

5.2 Subscription Models and Membership Sites

In the digital business, revenue generation is the ultimate goal, and in the quest for profitability, one strategy has emerged as a powerful cornerstone: subscription models and membership sites. These mechanisms, when well-executed, have the potential to not only sustain your business but propel it to new heights.

The Power of Subscription-Based Revenue

The very essence of subscription-based revenue lies in its reliability. In a world where revenue streams can be as unpredictable as the weather, having a steady flow of income can be a game-changer. Subscriptions provide this consistency. With subscription-based models, customers commit to periodic payments for access to your services or content. This arrangement offers numerous advantages for both the business and its customers.

For the business, the steady income from subscriptions offers financial stability, allowing for better planning, investment, and growth. The ability to predict cash flow, month after month, is invaluable. It enables you to set realistic goals, measure performance, and make informed decisions with confidence.

From the customer's perspective, subscriptions offer convenience and value. They gain access to a continuous stream of content, services, or products without the hassle of making repeated purchasing decisions. The subscription model fosters a sense of reliability and trust. Customers know what to expect, and this predictability can lead to long-term loyalty.

Creating Exclusive Content and Benefits
To build and maintain a successful subscription-based business, you must offer something truly special. Exclusive content and benefits are the linchpin of this strategy. Subscribers need a compelling reason to keep paying, and that reason is often found in what you provide exclusively to them.

Consider offering premium content that is not available to non-subscribers. This could be in the form of in-depth articles, videos, webinars, or tools that cater to the specific needs and interests of your subscribers. The key is to make your subscribers feel that they are getting superior value for their investment.

Another effective strategy is providing exclusive benefits. These can range from early access to new products, discounts on your merchandise, or even personalized customer support. The goal is to create a sense of belonging and privilege within your subscriber community. The more exclusive and tailored these benefits are, the stronger the bond you'll form with your audience.

Retaining and Nurturing Loyal Subscribers
Acquiring subscribers is an important step, but retaining them is the true challenge. The success of a subscription model depends on maintaining a base of loyal, satisfied subscribers. So, how do you ensure that your subscribers stick around?

Consistent, high-quality content and benefits are fundamental. Your subscribers should always feel that they are receiving their money's worth. Delivering on your promises is crucial to retaining trust and loyalty. Always strive to improve and innovate, as complacency can lead to subscriber attrition.

Engagement is another key factor. Interact with your subscribers, encourage their feedback, and create a sense of community. Hosting discussions, forums, or even live Q&A sessions can help foster a connection between you and your subscribers and among subscribers themselves.

Listen to your subscribers' feedback and adapt your offerings based on their input. Subscribers who feel heard are more likely to remain loyal. Additionally, consider implementing retention strategies like offering incentives for longer subscription commitments, such as annual plans. These not only provide financial benefits but also commit subscribers to your service for an extended period.

Subscription models and membership sites hold immense power in the world of digital business. They provide financial stability, foster customer loyalty, and create opportunities for growth. To harness this power, you must consistently deliver exclusive, high-value content and benefits while nurturing a strong sense of community and engagement. With these tactics, you can not only attract subscribers but also keep them for the long haul, ensuring the sustainability and prosperity of your digital business.

5.3 Leveraging Advertising and Sponsorships

In the world of digital business, finding effective monetization strategies that don't compromise user experience is both an art and a science. While building your zero-cost digital business, you'll inevitably reach a point where it's time to turn your hard work into revenue. This is where advertising and sponsorships can play a pivotal role.

Strategy for Ad Revenue Without Compromising User Experience

Advertising is a powerful avenue for generating revenue in the digital realm. However, the key to success lies in ensuring that the advertisements do not disrupt the user experience. Nobody appreciates intrusive ads that clutter the screen or interrupt their engagement with a website or application.

Here are practical strategies to leverage advertising without compromising user experience:

1. Native Advertising: Native advertising seamlessly integrates promotional content into the user experience, making it feel like a natural part of the platform. These advertisements are designed to match the style and format of the surrounding content, ensuring a non-disruptive experience for the user. By presenting ads in this subtle manner, you can engage your audience without causing annoyance.

2. Targeted Advertising: Personalization is the name of the game in the digital advertising world. Utilize user data and behavior tracking to serve ads that are relevant to the individual. When users see advertisements that align with their interests and needs, they're more likely to engage, and the ad feels less intrusive.

3. Ad Blocker Detection: Implementing ad blocker detection mechanisms allows you to educate users about the importance of advertising revenue for sustaining free content or services. You can kindly request users to disable ad blockers while offering an ad experience that's as unobtrusive as possible.

Attracting Potential Sponsors and Partners

When it comes to attracting potential sponsors and partners for your digital business, it's all about demonstrating the value and reach of your platform. Sponsors and partners can play a significant role in your revenue strategy, provided you approach them with a compelling proposition.

Here's how you can attract potential sponsors and partners:

1. Build a Strong Online Presence: Your digital business should have a robust online presence. This includes an engaging website, active social media profiles, and a thriving online community. When sponsors and partners see that you have a substantial and engaged audience, they'll be more interested in collaborating.

2. Create a Clear Value Proposition: Clearly define what you can offer to sponsors or partners. Highlight the benefits they'll receive, such as exposure to your audience, potential lead generation, or enhanced credibility through association with your brand.

3. Reach Out Strategically: Identify potential sponsors and partners whose values align with your business. Tailor your outreach to explain how their products or services complement your offerings. Personalize your communication to show that you've done your homework and understand their goals.

Negotiating Profitable Sponsorship Deals

Negotiating sponsorship deals is a critical skill in maximizing revenue for your digital business. It's not just about securing sponsors but doing so in a way that is mutually beneficial.

Consider these negotiation strategies for profitable sponsorship deals:

1. Know Your Worth: Before entering negotiations, have a clear understanding of the value you bring to the table. This includes your audience size, engagement metrics, and conversion rates. Use data to back up your claims.

2. Set Clear Objectives: Define your goals and what you want to achieve from the sponsorship. Whether it's increased brand exposure, a specific marketing campaign, or financial support, be explicit about your expectations.

3. Be Open to Customization: Flexibility can be a powerful negotiating tool. Be open to customizing sponsorship packages to meet the unique needs of your sponsors. This can make your proposal more appealing and align better with their objectives.

4. Establish Long-Term Partnerships: While one-off sponsorships can provide immediate revenue, long-term partnerships can offer stability and consistent support. Negotiate for ongoing relationships where both parties benefit from continued collaboration.

In the world of digital business, the balance between monetization and user experience is a delicate one. By implementing strategies for unobtrusive advertising, attracting potential sponsors and partners, and negotiating profitable sponsorship deals, you can navigate this balance successfully.

The key to sustainable revenue generation is aligning your monetization efforts with the needs and expectations of your audience while providing value to your sponsors and partners. With these strategies, you can drive profitability while maintaining a positive user experience in your zero-cost digital business.

Chapter 6: Scaling Your Zero-Cost Digital Business

6.1 Automated Systems and Tools

To gain success on digital business, scaling your venture is not just an option; it's a necessity. You've done the groundwork, carved your niche, and established your brand. Now, it's time to take it to the next level. How can you do that without draining your resources or exhausting yourself? The answer lies in the power of automation and the right selection of software and tools. This section is your gateway to a more efficient, productive, and sustainable digital business.

Implementing Time-Saving Automation

One of the most profound ways to scale your zero-cost digital business is through automation. Automation is the tireless workforce that never sleeps, never takes a break, and never makes a mistake. It can handle repetitive, time-consuming tasks, leaving you with more bandwidth to focus on high-value activities.

1: Identify Repetitive Tasks

Start by identifying the repetitive tasks in your daily operations. These might include sending out routine emails, managing social media posts, or processing customer inquiries. By pinpointing these tasks, you can make a clear plan for automating them.

2: Choose the Right Automation Tools

The market is flooded with automation tools and software, each claiming to be the best. Your task is to choose the right ones that align with your specific needs. Whether it's email marketing, social media management, or customer relationship management, there's an automation tool for nearly everything. Popular options include MailChimp, Hootsuite, and HubSpot.

3: Workflow Automation

A more advanced form of automation is workflow automation. This involves creating sequences of automated actions triggered by specific events. For instance, when a customer makes a purchase on your website, an automated workflow can send a thank-you email, update your inventory, and add the customer to your mailing list. Workflow automation minimizes manual intervention and reduces the chance of errors.

Selecting the Right Software and Tools

Software and tools are the gears that drive your digital business engine. The right choices can propel you forward, while the wrong ones can bog you down. When it comes to scaling your business, you need to be meticulous in selecting the right software and tools that suit your unique requirements.

1: Evaluate Your Needs

Before you embark on a software shopping spree, evaluate your business needs. What functions are crucial to your operations? What tasks need streamlining? Whether you require project management tools, accounting software, or design applications, a clear understanding of your needs will guide your selection process.

2: Cost Considerations

Remember, we're talking about a zero-cost digital business, so cost is a critical factor. Fortunately, many software options offer free versions or open-source alternatives. While the free versions may have limitations, they can often meet the basic needs of small to medium-sized enterprises.

3: User-Friendly Interfaces

The best software and tools are those that your team can use intuitively. Complex, overly technical software can lead to time wasted on training and troubleshooting. Opt for user-friendly options that allow your team to hit the ground running. This doesn't just save time; it can save you from costly mistakes.

Integrating and Optimizing Your Tech Stack

Now that you have your automation systems and the right software and tools, the next step is integrating and optimizing your tech stack. Your tech stack is the sum of all the technology you use in your business. Seamless integration ensures that all parts of your operation work harmoniously.

1: Centralized Data Management

Data is the lifeblood of a digital business. Whether it's customer information, sales figures, or market research, you need to centralize and manage your data effectively. Integration of tools and software ensures that data flows smoothly from one system to another. For instance, integrating your customer relationship management (CRM) software with your email marketing platform allows you to send targeted emails based on customer behavior.

2: Streamlined Communication

Communication is vital in a digital business, both internally and with customers. Integration of communication tools like Slack, Microsoft Teams, or even project management software with chat functions can streamline team collaboration. Externally, integrating chatbots with your website can provide instant customer support and responses, improving customer satisfaction.

3: Analytics and Reporting

Optimization isn't complete without the ability to track your progress and make informed decisions. Ensure that your software and tools come with robust analytics and reporting capabilities. This data can help you identify trends, assess the effectiveness of your strategies, and make data-driven decisions for further scaling.

Scaling your zero-cost digital business is all about efficiency, and automation, smart software and tool choices, and seamless integration are your allies in this quest. By implementing time-saving automation, selecting the right software and tools, and optimizing your tech stack, you'll find yourself with more time, fewer errors, and a business that's ready to expand without breaking the bank. Your digital empire awaits – it's time to seize the opportunities that lie ahead and make your business soar.

6.2 Outsourcing and Building a Virtual Team

When your zero-cost digital business begins to gain traction and your entrepreneurial dreams expand, scaling becomes the order of the day. To take your venture to the next level without breaking the bank, it's crucial to master the art of outsourcing and building a virtual team. This section will delve into this critical growth phase, where success hinges on your ability to delegate tasks effectively, identify and manage remote talent, and maintain seamless productivity and communication within a virtual workspace.

Delegating Tasks for Business Growth

As a digital entrepreneur, you're well aware of the importance of wearing multiple hats in the early stages of your venture. However, as your business starts to gain momentum, it becomes apparent that you can't do it all on your own. Delegation is the key to managing a growing workload effectively.

Delegating tasks involves entrusting specific responsibilities to other individuals or team members. This allows you to focus on high-impact activities, such as strategic decision-making and business development. It's not about relinquishing control but about optimizing your resources to achieve more.

Start by identifying the tasks that consume your time and can be handled by others. Prioritize based on urgency and impact. When delegating, ensure that you communicate your expectations clearly. A well-defined scope of work and milestones will help the person taking on the task understand what's expected. Regular follow-ups and feedback loops are essential to track progress and ensure alignment with your business goals.

Finding and Managing Remote Talent

In a zero-cost digital business, geographical boundaries are no longer limitations. Your potential talent pool isn't limited to a specific location; it's global. To scale effectively, you need to find and manage remote talent that can contribute to your business's growth.

Start by creating a clear job description outlining the role's responsibilities, skills required, and qualifications. Utilize online job platforms, freelance marketplaces, and social networks to reach a wide audience of potential candidates. Remember that remote work requires strong communication skills, self-discipline, and the ability to work independently. Assess these qualities during the hiring process.

Managing remote talent comes with its own set of challenges. While geographical separation can lead to isolation, it's essential to maintain a sense of connection and collaboration. Utilize digital communication tools, project management software, and regular video meetings to bridge the gap. Set clear expectations regarding working hours and deliverables, and establish a system for tracking progress.

Maintaining Productivity and Communication in a Virtual Workspace

As your team and operations span across different time zones and locations, maintaining productivity and effective communication is crucial. In a virtual workspace, technology becomes your closest ally.

Start by selecting the right tools for the job. Project management platforms like Asana, Trello, or Basecamp can help you track tasks and projects. Communication tools like

Slack, Microsoft Teams, or Zoom facilitate real-time conversations and video meetings.

Establish a structured routine. Determine daily or weekly check-ins to ensure that everyone is on the same page and that project timelines are met. Encourage transparency and open communication. In a virtual environment, problems and concerns need to be addressed promptly to avoid misunderstandings and delays.

Encourage a strong team culture despite physical separation. Team-building activities, virtual meetups, and shared goals help foster a sense of belonging. Celebrate successes and milestones, even if it's through a screen. A motivated and cohesive virtual team can work wonders for your business's productivity and overall success.

Scaling your zero-cost digital business requires not just ambition, but also the ability to adapt and leverage the virtual world's vast resources. Delegating tasks for growth, finding and managing remote talent, and maintaining effective productivity and communication are the cornerstones of this transformative process. Embrace the opportunity to build a dynamic, global team that drives your digital business toward new heights of success.

Chapter 6: Scaling Your Zero-Cost Digital Business

6.3 Strategies for Global Expansion

As your zero-cost digital business gains traction and becomes a well-oiled machine, the next logical step is to consider global expansion. The digital realm knows no geographical boundaries, and in a world interconnected by the internet, the potential for growth is boundless. However, venturing into international markets is not a step to be taken lightly. It requires a strategic approach that encompasses entering new markets and demographics, localizing content and services, and adapting to international regulations and cultural nuances.

Entering New Markets and Demographics

Expanding your digital business into new markets is a thrilling yet challenging endeavor. It opens up doors to an entirely fresh set of opportunities and customer demographics. Here's how you can effectively navigate this terrain:

1. Market Research is Paramount: Start by conducting in-depth research on the new market you intend to enter. Understand the local culture, consumer preferences, and market trends. What works in one market might not necessarily work in another.

2. Localized Marketing: Tailor your marketing strategies to align with the specific needs and interests of the new demographic. This might involve not just language translations but also cultural adaptations in your advertising campaigns.

3. Compliance and Legal Considerations: Each market comes with its own set of legal and regulatory requirements. Ensure that you are in full compliance with local laws, from taxation to data protection, before you make the leap.

Localizing Content and Services

When entering a new market, it's crucial to make your digital business resonate with the local audience. Localization extends beyond mere translation; it involves adapting your content and services to meet the unique preferences and expectations of your new customers:

1. Language Is Just the Beginning: Language localization is important, but also consider factors like currency, date formats, and units of measurement. The more seamless and native your digital offerings feel, the more likely you are to connect with your audience.

2. Cultural Sensitivity: Different cultures have different values, taboos, and sensitivities. Be mindful of cultural nuances, imagery, and content that might be perceived as offensive or inappropriate in your new market.

3. Customer Support: Provide customer support in the local language and time zone. Make sure your customers feel heard and understood.

Adapting to International Regulations and Cultural Nuances

Global expansion means navigating a diverse landscape of rules, regulations, and cultural norms. This is where thorough preparation is key:

1. Legal Counsel: It's highly advisable to seek legal counsel with expertise in international business law. They can guide you through the maze of regulations and ensure that you're in compliance with the legal requirements of the new market.

2. Cultural Competence: Your team needs to be culturally aware and competent. This goes beyond language skills. It means understanding the unwritten rules and norms that govern business conduct in a particular culture.

3. Local Partnerships: Building relationships with local businesses and entrepreneurs can be a game-changer. They can provide valuable insights, connections, and on-the-ground support. Collaborative efforts can open doors that might otherwise remain closed.

In a world where the internet is the gateway to international markets, global expansion is not a matter of "if" but "when." However, it's crucial to approach this with a well-thought-out strategy that considers the unique characteristics of each market, and respects their cultural and legal distinctions. With these strategies in place, you can successfully scale your zero-cost digital business across borders and continue to thrive on a global stage.

Chapter 7: Effective Customer Relationship Management

7.1 Building Customer Trust and Loyalty

Building and maintaining trust is the foundation of success in digital world. It's not just about making a quick sale; it's about fostering long-lasting relationships with your customers. As you stepping on your digital business venture, the strategies you employ to gain customer trust and implement effective loyalty programs will play a pivotal role in shaping the future of your enterprise.

Strategies for Gaining Customer Trust

Trust is the bedrock upon which you will construct your digital business. Without it, your prospects will remain just that—prospects, and not loyal customers. Trust can't be bought or bargained for; it must be earned, consistently and diligently.

1. Transparency Standard

Transparency is the linchpin of trust in the digital age. Your customers want to know who they're dealing with, what they're buying, and how their data is being used. Clearly articulate your business's identity, values, and policies. Let customers see the face behind the screen. Reveal your pricing structures, shipping policies, and terms and conditions without any hidden clauses or surprises.

Transparency isn't just a buzzword; it's a fundamental building block of trust.

2. Deliver on Promises

Every promise you make to your customers, no matter how seemingly small or insignificant, carries weight. If you guarantee same-day shipping, ensure it happens. If you promise a 24/7 customer support hotline, make sure it's available. Consistently delivering on promises, whether in product quality, service, or delivery, establishes a track record of reliability. This builds trust incrementally, one fulfilled promise at a time.

3. Listen to Your Customer

Communication is a two-way street. Don't just talk at your customers; listen to them. Create channels for feedback and take the time to genuinely understand their needs and concerns. Active listening demonstrates your commitment to their satisfaction. Engage with your audience through surveys, online forums, and social media platforms. When customers feel heard and valued, they're more likely to trust your brand.

Implementing Effective Loyalty Programs
Loyalty programs are the unsung heroes of digital businesses. They keep your customers coming back for

more and serve as a beacon of appreciation. Here's how to design and implement effective loyalty programs:

1. Rewards that Matter

It's not about the quantity of rewards; it's about their quality. Customers appreciate incentives that hold genuine value to them. Offering discounts, exclusive access to new products, or early-bird sales can be incredibly enticing. The key is to align your rewards with the preferences and desires of your target audience.

2. Simple and Accessible

Simplicity is a virtue in loyalty programs. The more straightforward and user-friendly your program is, the more customers will engage with it. Avoid convoluted point systems or complex redemption processes. Make it easy for customers to understand and participate.

3. Consistency and Recognition

Regularly engage with your loyal customers. Acknowledge their loyalty and show appreciation for their continued patronage. Personalized messages, birthday rewards, or exclusive content can go a long way in making customers feel valued. The consistency of recognition builds emotional bonds and strengthens loyalty.

Handling Customer Feedback and Complaints
No business is immune to the occasional hiccup or customer dissatisfaction. It's not about avoiding complaints, but rather about how you handle them. An effective digital business knows that complaints can be opportunities for improvement.

1. Timely Response

When a customer expresses dissatisfaction or raises an issue, prompt response is crucial. Acknowledge the problem, express empathy, and offer a solution or a path toward resolution. A delayed response can escalate the situation and erode trust.

2. Learn and Improve

Customer feedback, even when critical, is a goldmine of insight. Use it as a learning tool to improve your processes, products, and services. When customers see that you take their feedback seriously and act on it, their trust in your commitment to excellence deepens.

3. Build a Culture of Continuous Improvement

Instead of viewing complaints as nuisances, consider them as stepping stones to growth. Encourage employees to embrace a culture of continuous improvement. When every team member is dedicated to addressing customer concerns and iterating on solutions, trust flourishes.

In the digital business landscape, gaining customer trust and establishing loyalty is not a one-off task; it's an ongoing commitment. Transparency, consistency, and listening to your customers are foundational principles. Effective loyalty programs, when executed thoughtfully, serve as the glue that keeps your customers coming back for more. Lastly, handling feedback and complaints with grace and a commitment to improvement can turn challenges into opportunities for growth. Remember, trust isn't built overnight, but it can be nurtured and solidified through dedication and sincerity.

7.2 Customer Data and Personalization

In the world of digital business, the modern entrepreneur is armed with a potent weapon: customer data. Understanding the power of this data is the key to unlocking unparalleled success in your venture. In this section, we delve deep into the art of collecting and utilizing customer data, harnessing it to create personalized user experiences while striking that delicate balance with privacy.

Collecting and Utilizing Customer Data

Gone are the days of hunches and gut feelings. Today, data reigns supreme. The digital business landscape offers an abundance of information, and if you're not tapping into this goldmine, you're missing out on a competitive edge. Your customers are leaving digital breadcrumbs, and it's your duty to follow them.

Collecting customer data doesn't require a Sherlock Holmes level of detective work; it's about knowing where to look and how to gather it ethically. Start with the basics: website analytics, social media insights, and email subscriber information. These foundational sources provide valuable insights into customer behavior, preferences, and demographics.

Once you've got your hands on this treasure trove of data, it's time to put it to work. Data-driven decision-making is the hallmark of a successful digital business. Analyze the patterns, identify the outliers, and use this information to shape your strategies. Whether it's tailoring your content, refining your products, or optimizing your marketing, customer data gives you the laser focus needed to hit the bullseye.

Creating Personalized User Experiences

Imagine walking into your favorite coffee shop, and the barista knows your name, your preferred brew, and even suggests the latest pastry that suits your taste. It feels like they've read your mind, doesn't it? This level of personalization isn't just for the neighborhood cafe; it's the heart of the digital business game.

Personalization is the art of making your customers feel seen and heard in a digital world, where face-to-face interactions are scarce. It's about tailoring the user experience to suit individual preferences, making them feel like a valued part of your community. Personalization can take various forms, from recommending products based on past purchases to addressing customers by their first name in email communication.

Effective personalization is a careful blend of technology and empathy. Leverage the data you've collected to anticipate customer needs, but don't forget the human touch. It's a delicate balance. The goal is to enhance the user experience, not intrude on privacy. Customers should feel delighted, not stalked.

Balancing Personalization with Privacy
Privacy is a hot-button issue in the digital era. The line between personalization and intrusion is thin, and it's a line you can't afford to cross. Respecting your customers' privacy is not only ethical but also critical to maintaining their trust. A breach of privacy can lead to not only lost customers but also severe legal consequences.

To strike this balance, transparency is paramount. Make your data collection and usage policies crystal clear. Customers should willingly opt-in to sharing their data and understand how it will be used. An informed customer is more likely to trust your brand.

Anonymization is another strategy to protect privacy while personalizing user experiences. By stripping personally identifiable information from the data you collect, you can still glean valuable insights without risking privacy violations. Implement robust security measures to protect the data you store, and regularly audit your data management practices to ensure compliance with evolving regulations.

The management of customer relationships in the digital sphere is a multi-faceted challenge. It requires an understanding of the power of data, the art of personalization, and the respect for privacy. The success of your digital business hinges on your ability to leverage customer data while providing a seamless and personalized user experience. The fine line between personalization and privacy is your roadmap to building trust, loyalty, and enduring success in the digital age.

7.3 Customer Feedback and Continuous Improvement

Effective customer relationship management is the keystone to long-term success in digital world. It goes far beyond polite customer service and extends into a sophisticated understanding of your audience, their needs, and their evolving expectations. A vital component of this process is Customer Feedback and Continuous Improvement.

The Value of Feedback Loops

One of the cornerstones of an effective customer feedback strategy is the establishment of feedback loops. These loops are not just about hearing what customers have to say; they're about actively engaging with your audience and leveraging their insights to make meaningful changes.

Feedback loops create a direct channel of communication between you and your customers. They allow you to gain an unfiltered understanding of their experiences, needs, and pain points. This unfiltered nature is crucial because it enables you to peel back the layers of your business and see what truly lies beneath. It's akin to having a confidential conversation with your customers, where they freely express what works and what doesn't.

Imagine, for instance, you run a digital marketplace for handmade crafts. Your customers might have unique experiences when it comes to the buying and selling process. Through well-structured feedback loops, you can identify trends, pain points, and successes. This data can help you tweak your platform's interface, streamline transaction processes, and enhance the overall user experience.

It's essential to create a feedback culture where customers feel heard and respected. To do this, provide accessible channels for feedback, whether through email, surveys, or direct message communication. Beyond just soliciting feedback, though, act on it swiftly. Respond to concerns, fix glitches, and implement changes based on the insights received.

Analyzing and Acting on Customer Insights

Collecting feedback is just the beginning; the real magic happens when you transform those insights into actionable strategies. The key here is data-driven decision-making.

Suppose you're running an e-learning platform. You receive feedback from users that a particular section of your platform is confusing and that they struggle to find their coursework. To analyze this feedback effectively, you'd break it down. What part of the section is problematic? Is it a navigation issue, a design flaw, or unclear instructions? Once you've pinpointed the root cause, you can then take action to rectify it.

In this instance, you might conduct user testing sessions to understand the specific pain points. You could involve UX designers to revamp the section's interface and possibly create a more intuitive navigation system. The feedback isn't merely an echo of customer dissatisfaction; it's a guide to precision, showing you precisely where and how to make improvements.

Moreover, analyzing feedback also involves sifting through patterns and trends. Are there recurring themes in customer feedback? Are multiple customers voicing the same concerns? Identifying these patterns can direct your efforts, allowing you to prioritize and address the most significant pain points first.

By acting on customer insights, you're not just addressing issues – you're showing your audience that their opinions matter. You're building a rapport based on trust and credibility.

Continuous Improvement Strategies

Continuous improvement is not a one-time activity; it's an ongoing process that fuels the evolution of your digital business. The goal is simple: get better with each passing day, and in doing so, create a better experience for your customers.

To implement continuous improvement, it's essential to take a structured approach. Begin by setting up a feedback collection and analysis system that operates in real-time. The digital world moves fast, and you need to keep pace. The sooner you identify an issue, the quicker you can address it, preventing it from escalating.

Now, let's return to our e-learning platform. After implementing changes based on user feedback, you should continue to monitor the situation. Are users finding the revamped section easier to navigate? Are they expressing satisfaction with the improvements? If not, it's time to circle back and refine your strategy. This might involve additional user testing, surveys, or even direct interaction with users to get more detailed insights.

Alongside the specific feedback, keep a vigilant eye on industry trends and emerging technologies. Is there a new tool or feature that could benefit your users? By staying proactive in your approach, you not only maintain but also expand the value you offer.

Continuous improvement isn't only about fixing problems; it's about seizing opportunities. It's about cultivating a culture of innovation and adaptability that keeps your digital business ahead of the curve.

The process of effective customer relationship management, particularly in the realm of digital business, hinges on the symbiotic relationship between you and your audience. Feedback loops are your ears, providing you with valuable insights. Analyzing and acting on these insights is your heart, driving meaningful change. Continuous improvement strategies are your legs, propelling your digital business forward, step by step, to ensure it remains relevant, competitive, and customer-centric.

In the digital world, these principles are not optional; they are the essence of success. They embody the iterative process that leads to long-term customer loyalty and a thriving zero-cost digital business.

Chapter 8: Financial Management and Sustainability

8.1 Bootstrapping and Sustainable Finances

Money, as they say, makes the world go 'round. And in the realm of digital business, managing your finances effectively is the axis upon which your entire enterprise turns. In this section, we'll delve into the nitty-gritty of financial management and explore strategies for bootstrapping your business, ultimately preparing it for long-term financial sustainability.

Managing Cash Flow and Budgeting

Cash is the lifeblood of any business, digital or not. Without a steady stream of it, even the most promising ventures can wither and fade. The first step in financial success is understanding the art of managing cash flow. This entails creating a clear and comprehensive budget.

Budgeting is akin to having a roadmap for your financial resources. It involves categorizing your income and expenses, creating a clear picture of where your money is coming from and where it's going. For a digital business, this might include everything from server hosting fees to marketing costs.

Budgeting helps you anticipate financial fluctuations, prevents overspending, and ensures you're never caught off guard by unexpected expenses. It's a tool that not only grants you control over your finances but also provides a foundation for growth and stability.

Strategies for Bootstrapping Your Business

Bootstrapping, in the context of a digital business, is a badge of honor for entrepreneurs who are committed to building something from the ground up without external funding. It's an exercise in frugality, resourcefulness, and making every penny count.

One of the key strategies for bootstrapping is to minimize overhead costs. It involves scrutinizing every expense, no matter how minor it may seem. Can you find a more cost-effective hosting provider? Do you really need that premium software subscription, or are there open-source alternatives that will do the job just as well? By pinching those pennies and adopting a lean approach, you can stretch your budget far.

But bootstrapping isn't just about cutting costs. It's also about creative thinking. It's about leveraging your own skills and talents or those of your team. Can you handle your graphic design or content creation in-house instead of outsourcing? This not only saves money but can also cultivate a culture of multi-skilled individuals within your organization.

Another effective bootstrapping strategy is to generate revenue early on. Your digital business doesn't have to wait for a grand launch to start making money. In fact, it's often wiser to generate income from the get-go. Consider offering a minimal viable product (MVP) or an initial service at a modest fee. This not only starts the cash flow but also provides essential feedback from early customers, which can be invaluable for refining your offerings.

Bootstrapping can sometimes feel like tightrope walking. But as you embrace this financial discipline, you'll find that it breeds resilience and creativity, making you adept at adapting to challenges and, in the long run, building a more sustainable business.

Preparing for Financial Sustainability

Building a digital business that stands the test of time is not just about surviving today; it's about thriving for years to come. Financial sustainability is about setting your sights on the long term. It's a marathon, not a sprint.

Part of achieving financial sustainability is investing in the right places. As your business grows, don't shy away from smart, strategic expenditures that promise long-term returns. For instance, hiring a skilled team member or investing in better equipment can enhance your productivity and revenue.

It's also about building a financial cushion. Unexpected expenses are a fact of life in business, and having reserves to handle these bumps in the road can make the difference between a minor hiccup and a major setback. Whether it's through profit reinvestment or setting aside a percentage of your earnings, creating a financial safety net is a savvy move.

Moreover, diversifying your revenue streams is crucial for long-term sustainability. Relying solely on one source of income can be risky. Explore other income possibilities within your niche, such as affiliate marketing or the development of complementary products or services. This diversification hedges against potential downturns in any one area.

Lastly, remember that financial sustainability is not just about numbers; it's about maintaining your passion and enthusiasm for your business. As you navigate the financial complexities, it's essential to keep your entrepreneurial spirit alive. Your dedication and enthusiasm will fuel your journey toward a financially stable and successful digital business.

8.2 Raising Capital without Dilution

Raising capital is a fundamental aspect of scaling and sustaining your digital business. While many entrepreneurs opt for venture capital or angel investors, these options often entail giving up equity in your company. In this section, we'll explore alternative financing methods that allow you to secure the funds you need without diluting your ownership.

Alternative Financing Options

Traditional avenues like venture capital come with significant drawbacks. They often involve giving up a portion of your business, which can lead to a loss of control and decision-making power. This is where alternative financing methods step in.

Bootstrapping: One of the most challenging yet rewarding methods is bootstrapping. It means relying solely on your business's revenue to fund its growth. While this approach may require a longer journey to success, it keeps you in complete control of your venture. Bootstrapping demands discipline, frugality, and a commitment to maintaining a lean operation.

Revenue-Based Financing: Revenue-based financing is a unique approach that's gaining popularity. Here, you secure funds based on your future revenues. You agree to pay back a percentage of your income over time. This method provides you with the capital you need while allowing you to maintain ownership.

Business Loans: Traditional business loans from banks or online lenders are a viable option. These loans, secured based on your creditworthiness and business plan, give you access to funds without surrendering equity. Keep in mind that you'll need to repay the loan with interest.

Crowdfunding and Peer-to-Peer Lending
Crowdfunding and peer-to-peer lending platforms have disrupted the traditional fundraising landscape. These methods involve raising small amounts of money from a large number of people, eliminating the need to give up equity.

Crowdfunding: Websites like Kickstarter and Indiegogo offer a platform for you to pitch your business idea to the public. In return for their financial support, backers might receive early access to your product or other incentives. Crowdfunding has the added benefit of testing market demand for your product or service.

Peer-to-Peer Lending: Peer-to-peer lending platforms like Prosper and LendingClub connect borrowers with individual lenders. You can secure a loan from multiple lenders, each contributing a portion of the total amount you need. These loans often come with competitive interest rates.

Building Strategic Partnerships for Financial Support

Strategic partnerships can be a game-changer for your digital business. By collaborating with complementary businesses, you can secure both financial and non-financial support.

Co-Marketing Agreements: Partnering with another business can open new doors for your marketing efforts. Co-marketing agreements allow you to leverage each other's audience, expanding your reach without substantial expenses.

Joint Ventures: Joint ventures involve creating a new entity or project with a partner. This can be an effective way to pool resources and share both the costs and the rewards.

Strategic Alliances: Forming strategic alliances with businesses that share a similar target market can lead to financial support. These alliances can take various forms, from cross-promotions to shared resources.

Raising capital without dilution is entirely possible, even in the digital business landscape. Alternative financing methods like bootstrapping, revenue-based financing, and business loans allow you to maintain control of your venture. Crowdfunding and peer-to-peer lending platforms provide a way to secure funds from a broad range of supporters. Strategic partnerships, such as co-marketing agreements, joint ventures, and alliances, can be a valuable source of financial support.

The path to financial sustainability in your digital business requires careful consideration and a tailored approach. Your choice of financing method should align with your business goals and long-term vision. By exploring these alternative financing options and building strategic partnerships, you can secure the financial support you need to grow and sustain your digital business while retaining your ownership and control.

8.3 Profit Margins, Taxes, and Legal Considerations

When the realm of opportunity stretches as far as your creativity allows, it's crucial to keep an unwavering eye on the financial aspects of your venture. While your initial goal might have been to minimize costs and maximize revenue, the path to sustainable success also involves navigating profit margins, tax responsibilities, and legal considerations. Let's delve into the essential financial elements that will not only keep your business afloat but also propel it to new heights.

Maximizing Profit Margins

Profit margins are the lifeblood of any business, digital or otherwise. It's a measure of how efficiently your business is operating, reflecting the difference between your revenue and costs. In a zero-cost digital business, where your initial investment is minimal, your focus should be on optimizing these margins to ensure a healthy bottom line.

1. Cost Efficiency: One way to maximize profit margins is to be ruthless when it comes to cost efficiency. Keep a watchful eye on your expenses, and question each one's necessity. Reevaluate your operations regularly to identify areas where you can cut costs without sacrificing quality.

2. Pricing Strategy: Setting the right price for your digital product or service is a delicate balance. Pricing too high may deter potential customers, while pricing too low may hinder your profit margins. Research your competitors and your target market to find that sweet spot that ensures a healthy profit margin while remaining competitive.

3. Upselling and Cross-Selling: Often, the easiest way to increase your profit margins is to sell more to your existing customers. Offer complementary products or services,

bundle them together, or provide premium options for an additional fee. This approach not only enhances your revenue but also deepens your customer relationships.

Navigating Tax and Financial Compliance

Taxes and financial regulations are a constant in the world of business. While you may not be dealing with the complexities of a brick-and-mortar operation, zero-cost digital businesses are by no means exempt from their financial responsibilities. Navigating the tax and compliance landscape is not only essential for legal reasons but also for the long-term sustainability of your venture.

1. Tax Structure: Your choice of business structure will determine how you're taxed. Whether you're a sole proprietor, LLC, or corporation, each has its tax implications. Consult with a tax professional to select the structure that aligns best with your goals.

2. Record Keeping: Maintaining meticulous financial records is crucial. It not only helps you manage your finances but also ensures you're prepared for tax season. Use accounting software or hire a professional to help you keep track of income, expenses, and receipts.

3. Tax Deductions: Take full advantage of tax deductions available to you. In many regions, there are deductions for home office expenses, business-related travel, and equipment. Ensure you're aware of these deductions and claim them to reduce your tax liability.

Legal Protection and Risk Management

In the digital realm, legal issues and risks can take various forms, from intellectual property disputes to cyber threats. Ensuring the security and protection of your business is paramount to its sustainability.

1. Intellectual Property: Protect your digital assets. Copyright your content, trademark your brand, and ensure your intellectual property is secure. This safeguards your creations from infringement and helps you defend your business against copycats.

2. Terms of Service and Privacy Policies: If your digital business collects user data or operates a website, having comprehensive terms of service and privacy policies is non-negotiable. These documents not only establish transparency with your users but also protect you from potential legal disputes.

3. Cybersecurity: Cyber threats are a real and ever-present danger. Invest in robust cybersecurity measures to safeguard your data and that of your customers. Regularly update your software, employ encryption, and educate yourself and your team on safe online practices.

While it might be tempting to solely focus on the innovation and growth of your digital business, a clear understanding of your financial landscape, tax responsibilities, and legal protections is equally essential. Maximizing profit margins, staying compliant with tax regulations, and fortifying your legal defenses are the cornerstones of a sustainable and thriving zero-cost digital business.

By taking these financial considerations seriously and integrating them into your business strategy, you'll be better prepared to weather the challenges and complexities of the digital landscape. It's not just about launching your digital business; it's about ensuring it endures and prospers in an digital world.

Chapter 9: Customer Acquisition and Conversion Strategies

9.1 Organic Traffic and Content Marketing

The lifeblood of a thriving online business is undoubtedly organic traffic. The crux of acquiring that coveted audience begins with content marketing. To draw potential customers into your digital realm and, more importantly, to nurture them into loyal, paying patrons, you'll need a robust strategy that revolves around producing high-quality, relevant, and engaging content.

Building Organic Traffic through Content

Organic traffic is akin to gold dust in the digital landscape. It's the audience that stumbles upon your website or digital platform without the push of paid advertising. To attract this elusive but valuable crowd, your content must be magnetic.

Begin with understanding your audience. What are they seeking? What problems can you solve for them? Once you've unearthed these vital insights, craft content that provides solutions, answers questions, or offers insights.

Take a page from the playbook of successful digital businesses. They create content that resonates with their target audience, addressing their pain points and needs. It's not about flooding your platform with a sea of content; it's about producing content that's worth reading.

Content also needs to be optimized for search engines. That's where Search Engine Optimization (SEO) comes into play. Ensure that your content is well-structured, utilizing relevant keywords that your audience is likely to search for. This will increase your chances of ranking high on search engine results pages, making it easier for potential customers to find you.

Moreover, consistency matters. Regularly update your content to keep it fresh, relevant, and valuable. Search engines love fresh content, and so do your readers.

Content Marketing for Lead Generation

Once you've built organic traffic through valuable content, it's time to harness this influx of visitors into leads. Content marketing plays a pivotal role in this process.

Creating content that is not only informative but also enticing is key. It's about offering something in exchange for information. This can be in the form of e-books, whitepapers, webinars, or exclusive access to specific content. By doing so, you're effectively initiating a conversation with your audience, and they've shown their interest by willingly providing their contact information.

Moreover, content marketing is a potent tool for nurturing leads through the sales funnel. Tailor your content to different stages of the buyer's journey. For instance, awareness-stage content should educate and inform, while decision-stage content should be more persuasive and directly related to your product or service.

Successful digital businesses don't just throw content into the void and hope for the best. They use email marketing to deliver the right content to the right leads at the right time. By personalizing content delivery, you can establish a deeper connection with your audience and guide them through the conversion process.

Turning Leads into Customers

Gathering a plethora of leads is a remarkable feat, but it's not the end goal. You've got to convert those leads into paying customers.

This is where your content's nurturing power comes into play. By delivering valuable and relevant content at each stage of the buyer's journey, you're gently pushing leads toward a decision. But don't be overly pushy; let them make the decision on their terms.

Successful digital businesses employ lead scoring to identify the most promising prospects. By assigning scores to leads based on their behavior and interactions with your content, you can prioritize those who are most likely to convert.

Also, remember that a quick response to inquiries and personalized communication can make all the difference. Your potential customers want to feel valued and heard. Address their concerns, answer their questions, and offer support as they make their way toward a purchase.

Moreover, the user experience on your website or platform is critical. It should be seamless and intuitive. A complicated, confusing, or frustrating online journey can lead potential customers to abandon ship, no matter how promising your product or service.

The steps to customer acquisition and conversion begins with the creation of compelling, relevant, and well-optimized content. It's about understanding your audience's needs, nurturing them through the buyer's journey, and ultimately converting leads into loyal customers. In the realm of digital business, these strategies are your keys to success, and by mastering them, you can pave a path to sustainable growth and profitability.

9.2 Email Marketing and Lead Nurturing

In the digital world, where customer attention spans are shorter than ever, the ability to connect with your audience on a personal level has become a cornerstone of successful business. Email marketing and lead nurturing, when executed with precision and care, can be the linchpin that transforms casual visitors into loyal customers. In this chapter, we will delve into the pivotal aspects of email marketing, including building and segmenting your email list, crafting effective email campaigns, and lead nurturing for long-term customer retention.

Building and Segmenting Your Email List

Every successful email marketing campaign starts with a robust foundation: your email list. It's not just about amassing a colossal number of contacts; it's about cultivating a list of engaged and interested individuals. You see, your email list is not just a list; it's a dynamic community of potential customers.

1. Understanding Your Audience: The key to building a valuable email list lies in knowing your audience. Who are they? What are their needs, interests, and pain points? You'll want to create content that resonates with them and incentivizes them to join your email community.

2. Offering Value: People are protective of their inboxes, and rightly so. To earn a coveted spot, provide something of value in exchange for their email address. This might be a free e-book, exclusive access, or discounts. This initial offering is the cornerstone upon which your email list is constructed.

3. Segmentation for Personalization: Once you've amassed a sizable list, don't treat all your subscribers the same. Segment your list based on characteristics such as demographics, past behaviors, and preferences. By doing so, you can send tailored messages that resonate more deeply with each segment.

Crafting Effective Email Campaigns

Email marketing is a potent tool, but it's also a double-edged sword. If you bombard your subscribers with irrelevant or uninspiring content, you risk losing their interest and trust. Effective email campaigns strike the right balance, fostering engagement and driving conversions.

1. Compelling Subject Lines: The subject line is the gatekeeper of your email. It's the first thing your subscribers see, and it determines whether they'll open your message. Craft subject lines that are concise, intriguing, and relevant to the content inside.

2. Content that Adds Value: Your emails should be a source of value. Whether you're delivering educational content, exclusive offers, or updates, make sure it aligns with your subscribers' interests and needs. Keep it concise, scannable, and free from jargon.

3. Call to Action (CTA): Every email should have a clear and compelling CTA. Whether it's directing them to a product page, asking for feedback, or sharing your latest blog post, your CTA should be actionable and stand out visually.

Lead Nurturing and Customer Retention
Once you've captured your subscribers' attention and initiated a dialogue, the art of lead nurturing becomes the bridge to long-term customer retention.

1. Automated Sequences: Implementing automated email sequences ensures that your subscribers receive a series of targeted messages over time. These can include welcome sequences, onboarding sequences, and drip campaigns designed to guide your leads through the buyer's journey.

2. Personalization and Segmentation: As mentioned earlier, segmentation is pivotal, but personalization takes it a step further. Address your subscribers by name and tailor your content to their preferences. Leverage behavioral data to anticipate their needs and preferences.

3. Consistency and Value: Don't overwhelm your subscribers with daily emails. Maintain a consistent schedule, delivering content that provides value rather than bombarding them. You want them to anticipate your messages, not dread them.

4. Feedback Loops: Create a two-way conversation. Encourage feedback, questions, and replies from your subscribers. Address their concerns promptly and show them that you're not just a faceless entity but a partner in their journey.

Email marketing and lead nurturing, when executed with meticulous planning and personalized care, can be a potent force in your digital business strategy. Building and segmenting your email list sets the stage, crafting effective email campaigns drives engagement, and lead nurturing cements long-term customer retention. By understanding your audience, offering value, and fostering a sense of community, you can transform casual subscribers into loyal customers, all while adhering to the principles of personalization and value-driven communication.

9.3 Conversion Rate Optimization (CRO)

When success is often measured by the clicks, conversions, and sales generated on your website, Conversion Rate Optimization (CRO) is the secret sauce that can elevate your venture from merely existing to thriving. It's not a mysterious or elusive concept, but a systematic approach to refining your online presence to turn visitors into loyal customers. In this section, we will delve into the intricacies of CRO, focusing on optimizing landing pages and user experience, A/B testing, and utilizing CRO tools.

Optimizing Landing Pages and User Experience

Your landing page is your digital storefront. Just as a physical store needs to be inviting and easy to navigate, your landing page must be equally enticing and user-friendly. Here's how to optimize it for maximum impact:

1. Clarity is Key: Your landing page should communicate its purpose immediately. When visitors arrive, they should know what to expect. Remove any clutter, distractions, and unnecessary elements that might confuse or overwhelm them.

2. Concise and Persuasive Copy: Craft compelling and concise copy that resonates with your target audience. Explain how your product or service addresses their pain points, and what benefits they can expect.

3. Strategic Use of Visuals: The saying "a picture is worth a thousand words" holds true online. High-quality images and graphics can convey information more effectively than

text alone. Make sure your visuals align with your brand and message.

4. Simplify the User Journey: Make it easy for users to take the desired action. If it's a signup, purchase, or another conversion goal, minimize the steps needed to complete the process. Less friction means more conversions.

5. Mobile Optimization: With the increasing number of mobile users, ensure that your landing page is mobile-responsive. A seamless mobile experience is non-negotiable in today's digital landscape.

A/B Testing and CRO Tools

A/B testing is a fundamental component of Conversion Rate Optimization. It's the scientific method applied to the digital realm. A/B testing involves comparing two versions (A and B) of a webpage or element to determine which one performs better. Here's how it works:

1. Hypothesis Creation: Start with a clear hypothesis. What specific change are you testing, and what impact do you expect it to have? For example, if you hypothesize that changing the color of your call-to-action button will increase conversions, outline your expectations.

2. Test Implementation: Create two versions of the element you're testing. Version A (the control) remains unchanged, while version B (the variant) incorporates the proposed change. Use A/B testing tools like Google Optimize, Optimizely, or VWO to conduct these experiments.

3. Randomization and Data Collection: The A/B testing tool will randomly show version A or B to visitors and collect data on how each version performs. This data can include metrics like click-through rates, bounce rates, and conversion rates.

4. Statistical Analysis: Once you have a sufficient sample size, perform statistical analysis to determine if there's a significant difference in performance between the two versions. Statistical significance ensures your results are not due to chance.

5. Implementation of Findings: If the variant (Version B) outperforms the control (Version A), implement the changes permanently on your website. If not, return to the drawing board and refine your hypotheses.

Continuously Improving Your Conversion Strategies
Continuous improvement is the cornerstone of Conversion Rate Optimization. The digital landscape is dynamic, and what works today may not work tomorrow. Here are strategies for ongoing enhancement:

1. Data-Driven Decision Making: Always rely on data and analytics to guide your CRO efforts. Regularly analyze user behavior, conversion rates, and other relevant metrics. Identify trends and areas for improvement.

2. User Feedback: Your customers are a valuable source of insights. Collect and analyze user feedback through surveys, user testing, and direct communication. Their

input can uncover pain points and opportunities for enhancement.

3. Competitor Analysis: Stay informed about what your competitors are doing. Analyze their strategies, A/B testing results, and any innovations they implement. This can provide inspiration and a competitive edge.

4. Iterative Testing: CRO is not a one-time event. It's an ongoing process. Continue to test and iterate. What didn't work last month might work this month, and vice versa.

5. Team Collaboration: Collaborate with your team members, including designers, developers, marketers, and content creators. Everyone's expertise can contribute to the optimization process.

6. Stay Informed: Stay updated with the latest trends and best practices in CRO. The digital world is ever-evolving, and staying informed is crucial for maintaining a competitive edge.

Conversion Rate Optimization (CRO) is the engine that propels your digital business to new heights. Optimizing landing pages, conducting A/B testing, and consistently refining your conversion strategies are not mere suggestions; they are the lifelines of success in the online realm. By embracing these practices and continually improving, you can ensure that your digital venture thrives in a competitive and ever-changing landscape.

Chapter 10: Real-World Success Stories

10.1 Case Study 1 - The Story of Zendesk

Introduction to the Entrepreneur and Their Business

In the digital businesses, Zendesk is example one of entrepreneurial success. Founded by Mikkel Svane, Alexander Aghassipour, and Morten Primdahl in Copenhagen in 2007, Zendesk emerged as a pioneering force in the world of customer service and support software. The trio embarked on this journey with a simple but powerful idea: to revolutionize customer service with a cloud-based platform that would be accessible and affordable for businesses of all sizes.

Mikkel Svane, in particular, had a deep-rooted understanding of customer service. His own experiences as a customer, combined with the recognition of its significance in business success, served as the bedrock of Zendesk's mission. From humble beginnings in a small Copenhagen office, they embarked on a journey that would lead to the creation of a global software giant.

In the early days, Zendesk faced its share of challenges. Funding was scarce, and there was an intense need to differentiate from well-established competitors. However, Svane and his co-founders possessed unwavering determination and a willingness to adapt. Their vision was clear, and they continued to innovate with their cloud-based approach, making it an affordable solution that companies around the world could embrace.

Key Challenges and Their Solutions

One of the foremost challenges Zendesk confronted was the highly competitive landscape of customer service software. Established giants had already captured significant market share, and the prospects for a small startup in this arena seemed daunting. However, this challenge also brought opportunities.

Zendesk tackled this issue head-on by emphasizing simplicity. Their software was designed to be user-friendly, enabling businesses to set up and use it without extensive training. It was this emphasis on simplicity, coupled with affordability, that set them apart from their competitors. Businesses could start using Zendesk with little to no upfront cost, which was a game-changer for smaller enterprises.

Another challenge was the need to attract customers in a highly saturated market. Zendesk didn't have a massive marketing budget, so they relied on a bottom-up approach. They offered free trials, allowing potential customers to experience the benefits of their software firsthand. This approach, combined with a strong focus on customer feedback, allowed them to fine-tune their product according to market demands. Their commitment to customer satisfaction was not just a promise but a way of life for the entire company.

Perhaps the most significant challenge, though, was the need for scalability. As the company grew, Zendesk had to continuously adapt and ensure their platform could handle the increasing demands. Scalability was built into the core of their software, and this was vital in supporting their rapid growth.

Takeaways and Lessons from Their Success

Zendesk's success offers invaluable takeaways for aspiring digital entrepreneurs:

1. Simplicity Wins: Zendesk's emphasis on simplicity was pivotal to their success. In a world where complexity often reigns, their focus on user-friendliness set them apart.

2. Customer-Centric Approach: Zendesk's unwavering commitment to customer satisfaction, reflected in their free trials and feedback loops, is a lesson in the power of putting the customer at the center of your business.

3. Scalability Is Key: For a digital business to succeed, it must be able to scale with growing demand. Zendesk's forward-thinking approach to scalability ensured they could meet the needs of their expanding customer base.

4. Innovation Matters: The world of digital business is ever-evolving. Zendesk's journey is a testament to the importance of continuous innovation in staying relevant and competitive.

5. Start Small, Think Big: Despite facing stiff competition and budget constraints, Zendesk started small but had global aspirations. They leveraged affordability and accessibility to gradually conquer markets worldwide.

The story of Zendesk is not just an inspiring tale of entrepreneurial success but a practical blueprint for building a digital business from the ground up. Their focus on simplicity, customer-centricity, scalability, innovation, and the ability to start small while thinking big all contributed to their remarkable journey from a Copenhagen office to a globally recognized leader in customer service software. The Zendesk story proves that even in a fiercely competitive landscape, with the right approach and unwavering commitment, any digital entrepreneur can achieve remarkable success.

10.2 Case Study 2 - The Story of Zoho

Introduction to the Entrepreneur and Their Business:

In the digital entrepreneurship, there are a few names that stand out as examples of innovation, resilience, and success. One such name is Sridhar Vembu, the founder and CEO of Zoho Corporation. Zoho, a cloud-based software company, has not only achieved remarkable success but has also redefined the way businesses operate in the digital age.

Sridhar Vembu, a graduate of Princeton University with a Ph.D. in electrical engineering, embarked on a remarkable journey when he founded Zoho Corporation in 1996. What began as a small venture has grown into a global phenomenon, with over 60 million users and a suite of more than 40 cloud-based applications. Zoho's mission was clear from the outset: to provide affordable, high-quality software solutions for businesses, and Sridhar Vembu was determined to make that mission a reality.

Key Challenges and Their Solutions

The path to success is rarely without its obstacles, and Zoho was no exception. When Sridhar Vembu started the company, he faced numerous challenges, not the least of which was competition from industry giants. Many doubted that a small, independent player like Zoho could survive, let alone thrive, in the software industry. But Vembu's unwavering determination and unique approach to problem-solving allowed him to overcome these challenges.

1. Competitive Landscape: In the early days, Zoho faced stiff competition from established players in the software industry. Vembu realized that to succeed, he needed to differentiate Zoho from the competition. He did this by adopting a unique business model. While many software companies charged hefty licensing fees, Zoho offered a range of applications on a subscription basis, making their software affordable to businesses of all sizes. This pricing strategy disrupted the industry and attracted a growing customer base.

2. Bootstrapping and Self-Reliance: Unlike many startups that rely on external funding, Zoho was built with a strong emphasis on bootstrapping. Vembu believed in self-reliance and ensuring that the company's growth was sustainable without the pressures of external investors. This

approach allowed Zoho to remain focused on its long-term vision without compromising on product quality or user experience.

3. Talent Acquisition and Retention: Building a world-class team of software engineers and developers was another challenge that Sridhar Vembu faced. To address this, he established development centers in less urbanized areas of India, making it possible for the company to tap into a vast pool of talented engineers. By providing employees with opportunities for professional growth and emphasizing a culture of innovation and collaboration, Zoho not only attracted top talent but also retained it, creating a dedicated and motivated workforce.

Takeaways and Lessons from Their Success
The story of Zoho and Sridhar Vembu offers a wealth of valuable lessons for aspiring digital entrepreneurs:

1. Differentiate and Innovate: Zoho's success demonstrates the importance of differentiation and innovation. In a competitive landscape, offering a unique product or service can be a game-changer. Don't be afraid to challenge the status quo and disrupt traditional business models.

2. Embrace Self-Reliance: While external funding can be beneficial, Vembu's commitment to bootstrapping and self-reliance emphasizes the importance of building a sustainable business that doesn't compromise its long-term vision for short-term gains. This approach can empower you to maintain control and focus on your core mission.

3. Invest in Talent and Culture: Your team is your greatest asset. Building a diverse, skilled, and motivated team is essential for success. Create a culture of innovation, collaboration, and shared values to attract and retain top talent.

4. Affordable Accessibility: Making your products or services accessible to a broader audience can set you apart. Zoho's pricing strategy, offering high-quality software at an affordable price, played a significant role in its growth. Consider how you can adapt your pricing to meet the needs of a larger customer base.

5. Long-Term Vision: Success rarely happens overnight. Stay committed to your long-term vision and don't be discouraged by early setbacks. Zoho's journey from a small startup to a global corporation is a testament to the power of perseverance.

The story of Zoho and Sridhar Vembu is a compelling case study in digital entrepreneurship. It illustrates that with determination, innovation, and a focus on core principles, even a small startup can disrupt an industry and achieve global success. Their story serves as a reminder that in the world of digital business, success is attainable for those who dare to think differently and persevere through challenges.

10.3 Case Study 3 - The Story of Wix

Introduction to the Entrepreneur and Their Business

If you ever to build website, you must be ever heard of this company, Wix. Founded by Avishai Abrahami, Nadav Abrahami, and Giora Kaplan in 2006, Wix emerged as a pioneering force in the website-building and hosting industry. The trio of entrepreneurs envisioned a user-friendly platform that would enable individuals and businesses to create stunning websites with minimal technical knowledge.

Key Challenges and Their Solutions

When Wix first entered the digital landscape, it encountered several challenges that are familiar to many startups. The initial hurdle was convincing users that they could create professional-looking websites without a significant financial investment. This was a daring proposition at the time, as the prevailing sentiment was that quality websites demanded substantial capital.

Wix tackled this challenge head-on by offering a free, user-friendly website builder. This gave aspiring website creators the opportunity to experiment, explore, and realize the power of their platform without any financial commitment. It was a game-changer, as it not only removed the cost barrier but also simplified the technical aspects of website development.

However, the path was not without its share of struggles. As the user base grew rapidly, scalability became an issue. Wix needed to ensure that the platform remained robust and responsive, even with millions of users creating and hosting websites simultaneously. The solution lay in continuous investment in infrastructure, advanced technology, and strategic partnerships. This commitment to maintaining a top-tier hosting environment ensured that Wix could deliver on its promise of high-quality websites with zero-cost entry.

The evolution of Wix didn't end with just website creation. Another challenge the company faced was staying relevant in a dynamic online environment. With the rise of mobile devices, the demand for responsive and mobile-friendly websites grew exponentially. Wix met this challenge by developing a feature that automatically converted desktop websites into mobile-optimized versions. This innovation not only kept existing users satisfied but also attracted a new generation of mobile-first entrepreneurs.

The company also had to navigate the complex world of SEO (Search Engine Optimization) and e-commerce integration. Realizing that search engine visibility was vital for their users' success, Wix incorporated SEO tools and resources into its platform. Furthermore, they expanded their capabilities to support e-commerce, making it easier for small businesses to set up online stores.

Takeaways and Lessons from Their Success

The story of Wix offers several key takeaways for aspiring digital entrepreneurs:

1. Solve a Real Problem: Wix's success is grounded in its ability to address a common problem - the cost and complexity of website creation. By offering a free, user-friendly solution, they tapped into a massive market of individuals and small businesses looking for an affordable way to establish an online presence.

2. Embrace Innovation: Wix didn't rest on its laurels after creating a user-friendly website builder. The company continued to innovate, adapting to the changing needs of its users. It's a lesson in staying adaptable and responding to market demands.

3. Customer-Centric Approach: Wix prioritized its users' needs and ensured that the platform evolved in response to their feedback. This commitment to user satisfaction is a fundamental element of their success.

4. Partnerships and Infrastructure Investment: To support a growing user base, Wix invested significantly in its infrastructure and formed strategic partnerships. This approach allowed them to provide a reliable and scalable platform, which is crucial for retaining users.

5. Diversification and Expanding Services: As the digital business landscape changes, diversification can be a valuable strategy. Wix expanded its offerings beyond website building to include e-commerce and mobile

optimization, demonstrating that adaptability and the ability to meet different needs can drive growth.

The story of Wix is an inspiring tale of how a trio of entrepreneurs identified a challenge, devised a revolutionary solution, and evolved with the digital landscape. Their focus on user satisfaction, innovation, and adaptability makes them a prime example of digital business success. Entrepreneurs can draw valuable lessons from Wix's journey and apply them to their own ventures, forging a path toward success in the dynamic world of digital business.

Chapter 11: Digital Business in the Future

11.1 Emerging Trends in Digital Business

Digital business is a dynamic and ever-evolving field. As we look into the future, we're faced with exciting possibilities and challenges that will redefine the landscape. In this section, we'll delve into the future trends of the digital business world, the opportunities presented by emerging technologies, and the imperative of staying ahead of the curve.

Future Trends in the Digital Business Landscape

The digital business landscape is undergoing a significant transformation, and being aware of the upcoming trends is crucial to staying competitive. Here are some key trends to watch out for:

1. AI-Powered Personalization: Artificial intelligence and machine learning are becoming increasingly sophisticated, allowing businesses to deliver highly personalized customer experiences. This trend will continue to grow, and businesses that harness the power of AI to tailor their products and services to individual preferences will gain a substantial competitive edge.

2. Blockchain for Trust and Transparency: Blockchain technology is not just about cryptocurrencies; it has the potential to revolutionize various industries by providing unparalleled trust and transparency. From supply chain management to smart contracts, blockchain will continue to

shape the way businesses operate and interact with their customers and partners.

3. Sustainability and Social Responsibility: The global focus on sustainability and social responsibility is not a passing trend; it's a fundamental shift in consumer expectations. Companies that actively embrace sustainable practices and align with societal values will resonate more with their audience. Sustainability is no longer a choice but a necessity for long-term success.

4. Remote Work and Decentralization: The COVID-19 pandemic accelerated the adoption of remote work, and this trend is here to stay. Digital businesses will need to adapt to remote workforces, find new ways to collaborate, and ensure the security of distributed operations.

5. Data Privacy and Security: With the proliferation of data breaches and increasing awareness about data privacy, consumers demand greater transparency and control over their personal information. Compliance with data protection regulations will become more stringent, and businesses will need to invest in robust data security measures.

6. Augmented Reality (AR) and Virtual Reality (VR): AR and VR technologies are moving beyond gaming and entertainment. They offer exciting possibilities for enhancing customer experiences, from virtual showrooms to interactive product demonstrations. Businesses that can harness the potential of AR and VR will create immersive and engaging experiences for their customers.

Opportunities in Emerging Technologies

Emerging technologies are the building blocks of the digital future. To seize opportunities and remain competitive, it's essential to understand and leverage these technologies:

1. 5G Technology: The rollout of 5G networks promises lightning-fast internet speeds and low latency, opening up possibilities for real-time communication and the Internet of Things (IoT). Digital businesses can explore applications in areas such as augmented reality, telemedicine, and smart cities.

2. Internet of Things (IoT): The IoT continues to expand, with connected devices making their way into homes, industries, and cities. Businesses can tap into IoT for data collection, process optimization, and predictive maintenance, creating new revenue streams and enhancing customer experiences.

3. Edge Computing: Edge computing, which brings computation and data storage closer to the source of data generation, enhances real-time processing. This is particularly valuable for applications in autonomous vehicles, smart infrastructure, and industrial automation.

4. Quantum Computing: While still in its infancy, quantum computing has the potential to solve complex problems that are currently beyond the capabilities of classical computers. It may revolutionize fields like cryptography, materials science, and drug discovery.

5. Biotechnology and HealthTech: Advances in biotechnology and health technology are poised to transform healthcare and wellness. Digital businesses can explore opportunities in telemedicine, wearable devices, and personalized health solutions.

Staying Ahead of the Curve

In this fast-paced digital business landscape, staying ahead of the curve is not just a competitive advantage but a survival necessity. Here are practical steps to ensure you remain at the forefront:

1. Continuous Learning: Commit to ongoing education and skill development. Keep abreast of industry news, trends, and emerging technologies by enrolling in online courses, attending webinars, and participating in industry forums.

2. Adaptability: Embrace change and be open to adapting your business model to accommodate new technologies and market shifts. Be willing to pivot when necessary.

3. Network and Collaborate: Forge strategic partnerships and collaborate with experts and like-minded businesses. Collaborative efforts often lead to innovation and mutual growth.

4. Experimentation: Don't fear failure; instead, view it as a learning opportunity. Experiment with new technologies, strategies, and business models to discover what works for your specific niche.

5. Customer-Centricity: Keep your customers at the center of your decisions. Understand their evolving needs and preferences, and tailor your products and services accordingly.

6. Risk Management: As you embrace emerging technologies, be aware of associated risks. Develop risk management strategies and ensure data security, compliance, and business continuity plans are in place.

The digital business world is an ever-evolving ecosystem. To succeed, you must be proactive, adaptable, and forward-thinking. By keeping an eye on emerging trends, embracing new technologies, and staying ahead of the curve, you'll position your business for long-term success in this dynamic environment. The future of digital business is bright, but it belongs to those who are ready to seize it.

11.2 The Role of Sustainability and Corporate Social Responsibility

Sustainability and Corporate Social Responsibility (CSR) are not mere empty words; they represent the fundamental pillars upon which the future of digital business is built. In the pursuit of long-term success, digital entrepreneurs must not only focus on profitability but also consider their impact on society and the environment. In this section, we delve into the crucial aspects of sustainability, the implementation of CSR initiatives, and the art of building a socially responsible digital brand.

Integrating Sustainability into Your Business Model
To truly embrace sustainability within your digital business, it is essential to ingrain it into the very fabric of your business model. Sustainability is not a standalone concept but an inherent part of how you operate and grow your venture.

Sustainability begins with conscious decision-making. It means choosing eco-friendly alternatives, reducing waste, and optimizing resource usage. For instance, consider the energy you consume in your digital operations. Transitioning to renewable energy sources, optimizing server energy efficiency, and reducing digital waste through responsible data management all contribute to a sustainable business model.

Additionally, sustainability extends to your supply chain. Evaluating your suppliers and ensuring that they adhere to ethical and environmental standards can make a significant difference. By sourcing from responsible partners and supporting local and sustainable businesses, you become a part of the solution.

Beyond these practical measures, it also involves fostering a culture of environmental responsibility within your organization. Educate your team on sustainability and empower them to integrate these values into their daily tasks. Small steps, such as reducing paper usage, minimizing travel, or encouraging remote work, can collectively make a substantial environmental impact.

Implementing CSR Initiatives

Corporate Social Responsibility (CSR) initiatives encompass a broader perspective of the impact your digital business has on society. While sustainability predominantly focuses on environmental aspects, CSR includes social and ethical dimensions.

CSR involves giving back to the community and actively participating in philanthropic endeavors. This could be in the form of donations, volunteering, or partnerships with charitable organizations. Engaging in CSR initiatives not only benefits the society at large but also enhances your brand's reputation and fosters a sense of social responsibility among your employees.

Furthermore, CSR encompasses ethical practices within your business. Ensuring fair wages, equal opportunities, and diversity in your workforce demonstrates a commitment to social justice. It is also about the responsible use of customer data, maintaining data privacy, and adhering to ethical marketing practices.

CSR initiatives also extend to promoting transparency in your operations. Being open and honest about your business practices and finances fosters trust among your customers. Clearly communicating your CSR efforts and their impact is essential. Your audience should know how their support contributes to a better world.

Building a Socially Responsible Digital Brand

A socially responsible digital brand is more than a label; it's a commitment. It's a promise to your customers, employees, and the world that your business is driven by values beyond profit. Building such a brand requires a comprehensive approach.

Start with your mission and values. A socially responsible brand's mission statement is a beacon that guides every decision and action. Make it clear that your business is dedicated to making a positive impact, be it through eco-friendly practices, ethical business conduct, or community engagement.

Consistency is key. Your brand's identity, messaging, and actions should align with your commitment to social responsibility. For example, if your brand supports a cause, ensure that your content and marketing materials reflect this support. Walk the talk.

Engaging your audience is vital. Encourage them to be part of your socially responsible journey. Share your CSR initiatives and sustainability efforts through your digital channels. Invite your customers to participate in your philanthropic endeavors, such as donating to a cause for every purchase they make.

Accountability cannot be overstated. Your brand should be open to feedback and willing to improve. If mistakes are made or your CSR initiatives face challenges, acknowledge them, learn from them, and take action to rectify them.

The future of digital business is undeniably intertwined with sustainability and corporate social responsibility. These are not just trends; they are prerequisites for lasting success. By integrating sustainability into your business model, implementing meaningful CSR initiatives, and building a socially responsible brand, you not only ensure the longevity of your digital venture but also contribute to a better, more responsible, and more ethical world. It's more than just good business; it's a moral obligation in our ever-connected, digital age.

Conclusion

Taking Action: Your Roadmap to Success

In the preceding chapters, we've already learned on a pragmatic and data-driven exploration of how to build a zero-cost digital business from scratch and turn it into a thriving enterprise. But now that we've covered the critical strategies, principles, and case studies, it's time to switch gears and talk about the future, particularly your future.

This chapter isn't just a conclusion, but rather the beginning of a new phase. We're transitioning from learning to implementation, from theory to practice. It's about taking the knowledge you've gained and transforming it into concrete actions that will shape the trajectory of your digital business. Let's dive right in.

Setting Post-Book Action Plans

You've invested your time and effort in absorbing the insights presented in this book, and now it's time to put that knowledge to work. The first step in ensuring your post-book success is to create an action plan tailored to your unique business aspirations.

Action Point 1: Define Your Goals

Begin by defining your specific goals. What do you aim to achieve in the next quarter, year, or even five years? Your goals should be SMART (Specific, Measurable,

Achievable, Relevant, and Time-bound) and aligned with your digital business's overarching mission.

Action Point 2: Break Down Goals into Actionable Steps

Once you've set clear goals, break them down into smaller, manageable steps. Think of these as milestones or checkpoints on your path to success. Having these smaller steps will make your journey less overwhelming and more achievable.

Action Point 3: Develop a Timeline

Create a timeline that outlines when you expect to reach each milestone. This timeline is your roadmap, a visual guide that keeps you on track and accountable.

Action Point 4: Allocate Resources

Assess the resources you need to reach your goals. This may include time, budget, talent, or tools. Make sure you allocate resources wisely to support your plan.

The Importance of Continuous Learning and Improvement

In the digital business, one thing is certain: change is constant. To stay ahead, you must make continuous learning and improvement an integral part of your routine.

Action Point 1: Embrace Lifelong Learning

The digital world doesn't stand still, and neither should you. Commit to lifelong learning. Stay updated with industry trends, emerging technologies, and best practices. This could involve reading books, attending webinars, or enrolling in online courses.

Action Point 2: Experiment and Adapt

Don't be afraid to experiment. Digital businesses that innovate and adapt are the ones that thrive. Whether it's testing a new marketing strategy or refining your product based on customer feedback, continuous improvement is key.

Action Point 3: Analyze Data and Metrics

Data is your friend. Regularly analyze the data and metrics related to your digital business. Understand what's working and what isn't. Use this data to make informed decisions and refine your strategies.

Building a Network of Support and Collaboration

One of the most significant assets you can cultivate in your digital business journey is a network of support and collaboration. This network can be your sounding board, your source of inspiration, and your safety net.

Action Point 1: Seek Mentors and Advisors

Look for experienced individuals who can mentor you and provide guidance. Their insights can be invaluable. Don't underestimate the power of a well-chosen mentor.

Action Point 2: Join Online and Offline Communities

Digital business isn't a solitary endeavor. Join online forums, social media groups, and local meetups related to your niche. Connect with like-minded individuals, share your experiences, and learn from others.

Action Point 3: Collaborate with Partners

Collaboration can expand your reach and bring new opportunities. Seek out partnerships with businesses that complement yours. Collaborative efforts can lead to co-marketing, joint ventures, or the creation of new products or services.

The digital business landscape is a vast, dynamic realm brimming with possibilities. As you embark on your post-book journey, remember that the path to success is not a single, linear trajectory. It's a series of steps, adjustments, and reevaluations that ultimately lead you closer to your goals.

By setting clear action plans, embracing continuous learning, and cultivating a network of support and collaboration, you are not merely following a blueprint; you're crafting your own success story. The future of your digital business lies in your hands, and the possibilities are boundless. It's time to take action, learn, grow, and create a thriving digital enterprise. Your future begins now.